Agriculture, the Countryside and Land Use

AN ECONOMIC
CRITIQUE

J. K. BOWERS and
PAUL CHESHIRE

Agriculture, the Countryside and Land Use

AN ECONOMIC CRITIQUE

METHUEN
LONDON AND NEW YORK

First published in 1983 by
Methuen & Co. Ltd
11 New Fetter Lane, London EC4P 4EE
Published in the USA by
Methuen & Co.
in association with Methuen, Inc.
733 Third Avenue, New York, NY 10017

Printed in Great Britain by
Richard Clay (The Chaucer Press) Ltd
Bungay, Suffolk

British Library Cataloguing in Publication Data

Bowers, J. K.
Agriculture, the countryside and land use.
1. Agriculture and state—Great Britain
I. Title   II. Cheshire, Paul C.
338.1'84   HD1927

ISBN 0-416-31830-4 Pbk

Library of Congress Cataloging in Publication Data

Bowers, J. K.
Agriculture, the countryside and land use.

Includes bibliographical references and indexes.
Supt. of Docs. no.: NF 2.2:Ar7/4
1. Agriculture and state—Great Britain—History—
20th century. 2. Land use, Rural—Government policy—
Great Britain—History—20th century. 3. Agricultural
pollution—Great Britain—History—20th century.
I. Cheshire, P. C.   II. Title.
HD1927.B68 1983   338.1'8   83-13069
ISBN 0-416-31830-4 (pbk.)

Contents

List of figures

List of tables

Preface and acknowledgements

This book started as a conversation when the authors were working at the National Institute of Economic and Social Research in 1967. The basic ideas have been developed and extended through a series of outlets since then but, as both authors have been primarily engaged in research in other fields of economics, the book has seen a long gestation; it might fairly be seen, indeed, as overdue.

What we have now produced is intended as a work of political economy; a book which combines academic research with persuasion. We think that both the evidence we have assembled and the analysis of that evidence demonstrate beyond reasonable doubt that there is something very wrong indeed with both the level and form of agricultural subsidies. And having made that assessment (as have many other observers in the last thirty years) we wish to persuade our readers of the case. Our intention and hope is to reach the general reader as well as, and indeed more than, the professional economist. Consequently we have tried to use plain English, avoiding jargon wherever possible.

With a book that has been so long in preparation it is inevitable that we are indebted to more people than we can now remember. In the early days we had many helpful discussions with Christie Davies, Eric Jones and Ray Thomas, subsequently with John

Andrews, Doug Boyd and Gwynn Williams. We should also thank the Open University for allowing us to incorporate a modified version of material that first appeared in their course. More recently we have had help from colleagues at Leeds and at Reading. We should like to thank C. J. Black, James Hopkinson, Alan Swinbank and Ivy Smith for reading and commenting on much of the manuscript. Responsibility for what is now written rests of course wholly with us.

The tedious task of typing and re-typing the manuscript has been performed admirably by Teresa Brier and Beryl Jones, to whom we give our grateful thanks.

Finally it should be made clear that neither author has any connection with departments of agriculture or agricultural economics in our respective universities.

Universities of Leeds   *John Bowers and*
and Reading   *Paul Cheshire*
March 1983

List of abbreviations

AHGS   Agriculture and Horticulture Grants Scheme
CAP   Common Agricultural Policy
CPRE   Council for the Protection of Rural England
DMV   Deserted Medieval Village
EAGGF   (FEOGA) European Agricultural Guidance and
   Guarantee Fund
EDC   Economic Development Committee
EEC   European Economic Community
IDB   Internal Drainage Board(s)
MAFF   Ministry of Agriculture, Fisheries and Food
MCA   Monetary Compensatory Amounts
NCC   Nature Conservancy Council
NFU   National Farmers' Union
RSPB   Royal Society for the Protection of Birds
SMD   Standard Man Day
SSSI   Sites of Special Scientific Interest
UA   Units of Account
WA   Water Authority
WHO   World Health Organization
YHA   Youth Hostelling Association

There once were brooks sweet whimpering down the vale:
The brook's no more — kingcup and daisy fled;
Their last fall'n tree the naked moors bewail,
And scarce a bush is left to tell the mournful tale . . .

The thorns are gone, the woodlark's song is hush,
Spring more resembles winter now than spring,
The shades are banish'd all — the birds have took to wing.

There once were lanes in nature's freedom dropt,
There once were paths that every valley wound —
Inclosure came, and every path was stopt;
Each tyrant fix'd his sign where paths were found,
To hint a trespass now who cross'd the ground:
Justice is made to speak as they command; . . .
Ye fields, ye scenes so dear to Lubin's eye,
Ye meadow-blooms, ye pasture-flowers, farewell!
Ye banish'd trees, ye make me deeply sigh —
Inclosure came and all your glories fell.
E'en the old oak that crown'd yon rifled dell,
Whose age had made it sacred to the view,
Not long was left his children's fate to tell;
Where ignorance and wealth their course pursue,
Each tree must tumble down — old 'Lea-close Oak', adieu!

From *The Village Minstrel* (1821) by John Clare

1

Introduction

Danebury Down in Hampshire used to be regarded as classic chalkland habitat, a downland pasture interspersed with hawthorn scrub. On one side lay a famous 19th century racecourse and above it the remains of an Iron Age hill fort. Many of the fast vanishing birds of southern England bred in this area: red-backed shrikes, woodlarks, redstarts, long-eared owls and hobbies. The flora excellently typified the variety of chalkland plant life and included several species of orchid. In 1960 it was ploughed up and now the birds and plants have vanished. The racecourse, which had survived the urgent need for land in two world wars, succumbed to the agricultural policies of the 1960s and that was ploughed up also. The fort alone was preserved, partly through the intervention of the county council and partly because it was difficult to plough.

We originally wrote this in 1969.[1] Since then something of substance has changed. The destruction of the British countryside has extended from lowland England deep into the West Country, to the uplands of England and Wales and to the wetlands. This process has, as we discuss in Chapter 2, been documented in publications by, for example, the Nature Conservancy Council and the Countryside Commission; it has been documented more polemically by Marion Shoard[2] and others. But it has continued and accelerated. One of us returned to a favourite spot in the Welsh mountains last summer, a pool in a brook in a hidden valley 530 metres above sea level. The growing season there is very short and the land has been used for rough grazing for sheep for many years. But with the help of a 70 per cent grant this upland area was now being drained and fenced, soon to be ploughed, seeded and fertilized, with the help of yet further subsidies. The brook just below the pool was now channelled through four 45 cm concrete pipes over which went a concrete bridge for the new 50 per cent grant-aided farm road. This ran for more than 1.5 km over the moorland.

Developments such as these are not the result of some inevitable technical progress or pressure of population on resources. They result solely and simply from the economic insanity of agricultural policies and support measures. What the land produces is subsidized twice over by import levies and hill livestock subsidies. The costs of the 'improvements' are mostly met by public money and the value of what was there before, a beautiful trout-filled brook and a valley full of wild plants and birdlife, enters into nobody's financial calculations.

The changes in the countryside which these examples typify and which are now well-documented and much decried, though still continuing, stem from a trend in British agriculture apparent ever since the Second World War. In a word this trend may be described as intensification. It has taken several different forms, each more significant at particular times. There has been the movement towards monoculture and away from the old mixed farm. This together with the increase in arable and temporary grass at the expense of permanent pasture and the elimination of hedges has created over much of lowland England a landscape of increasing monotony and dangerous potentialities. With that trend has increasingly gone the banishment of livestock from the fields to covered yards and specialized intensive units. This process of tillage, especially cereal, expansion and the rise of specialization was almost complete by the end of the 1960s. By then the area of barley had increased sixfold since before the war. Overall the area of wheat and barley in England and Wales increased by 87 per cent from 1947 to 1966, and that of temporary grass increased by 5 per cent. The detailed case study in Chapter 3, of a 20 square kilometre area of southern England on the Berkshire downs, traces the local impact of these and other changes. The traditional mixed farm with its economies of joint production and inbuilt advantage in the face of individual product price fluctuations has been swept away. In the four years from 1963 alone, numbers declined by 33 per cent.

It was swept away not because economies of joint production had ceased to exist or product prices on uncontrolled world markets had ceased to fluctuate; far from it. As was testified by the increasingly frequent sight of burning straw in the fields of specialized cereal growers; or lorries loaded with straw from the western fringes of the cereal area, *en route* for the specialized livestock farms of the west; or the stinking slurry ponds and their surrounding rank vegetation and polluted waterways of the intensive livestock units; or the fish, poisoned by deoxygenation of waterways, heavy with leached artificial fertilizers; these inter-relationships were still there. And, as is argued in Chapter 5, the expansion of the EEC with its reliance on import levies and controlled prices, made world price fluctuations more extreme.

Traditional mixed farming gave way not to updated mixed farming but to capital intensive specialist farming, largely as the result of policy designed for that end. By subsidizing output prices, farming became more profitable so land prices rose and intensification became necessary for survival. Farm sizes were regarded by policymakers virtually as given, so capitalization and the search for economies of scale led to specialization. Heavy investment in combine harvesters and handling and drying equipment could only appear justified if the farmer had a very much larger area of cereals. This could be done by expanding the farm size whilst continuing with a number of enterprises, or it could be done by specialization. Specialization, with its loss of joint economies and higher environmental costs, was the route taken.

Since the late 1960s the area of arable has stabilized and the rate of growth of the wheat and barley area, although it was continued, has moderated. Intensification has now taken the form of a continuing expansion of cereals, especially wheat, and of one or two other crops such as sugar beet and oilseed rape, a convenient break crop in cereal. (The evidence of the Permanent Secretary of MAFF to the House of Commons Agriculture Committee (*Minutes of Evidence 11 November 1982*) is extremely revealing: 'if someone had asked me in 1972 whether oilseed rape would be an important crop in this country I would have said "No. There is no way we can compete with the United States or the Third World with oilseeds." Then the European Community . . . puts a subsidy of about 100 per cent on the import value of the commodity. It is now a leading and highly profitable crop.') There has also been a continuing increase in livestock numbers, cattle up by 7 per cent and sheep up by 19 per cent. This has been accommodated by higher stocking rates for sheep and more intensive methods for cattle. For cattle, husbandry methods are increasingly following the lead of poultry and pigs as they come out of the fields and go into intensive, highly capitalized, units.

These changes have brought about the detrimental effects on the countryside discussed in detail in the early chapters of this book. They have destroyed important wildlife habitats. They have damaged the beauty of the British landscape, itself the creation of generations of farmers practising agricultural techniques in harmony with their environment. They have caused serious environmental pollution, threatening wildlife and, at the extreme, causing one water authority to import bottled, nitrate-free, drinking water supplies for young babies. They have reduced the amenity and recreational value of the countryside and made very much more serious the conflict between farmers and the growing recreational use of the countryside. And, as we show in Chapters 4, 5 and 6, they have gobbled up inordinate quantities of scarce resources.

It must be acknowledged that with rising labour costs and falling real costs of capital, combined with technical progress, change would have occurred. But the changes just discussed are the essential creature of agricultural policy both in and out of the EEC.

In the period following the Second World War, the aims of policy were greater self-sufficiency in food, following the wartime experience, and 'proper remuneration' for farmers and workers in agriculture. It is interesting to note in passing that whilst farmers' incomes relative to those of other workers have increased by a factor of 2.5, those of their workers have increased by only 1.4. The aims led to, first, guaranteed prices well above those in the world market and then, in the early 1950s, to the introduction of production grants on certain inputs. Although the particular emphasis changed through time, its elements have survived our entry into the EEC and adoption of the Common Agricultural Policy (CAP) regime of support. Thus, since the Second World War, the financial tune to which farmers have danced has been played in Whitehall – and now Whitehall and Brussels – and its strains have not reflected either real resource costs or the social value of output but the prejudices of the Ministry of Agriculture, Fisheries and Food (MAFF) and the pressure group politics of the farmers' unions.

The mechanisms whereby this manipulation of perceived prices and costs have brought about the changes in agriculture have been at the same time both simple and subtle. And all the time the music of financial manipulation has been reinforced with the constant exhortation of the policy's barkers: the agricultural advisory services. The simple routes are easy to see. Let us take just the example of the increase in specialization in cereals with its concomitant hedgerow grubbing and loss of wildlife habitat and public access. Through high guaranteed prices, cereal production was made more profitable both absolutely and relatively. Through grants the cost of machinery was reduced; artificial fertilizers were made available at half their price; and ploughing of permanent pasture and hedgerow grubbing were directly subsidized so that the real cost to the farmer, with tractors and labour more or less unoccupied in the slack season, was often zero.

The more complicated mechanisms were that financial induce-ments for farm amalgamations were trivial whilst the pressures for amalgamation were much reduced by the level of subsidy. The reduced cost of specialized capital led to the logical choice of a specialized enterprise. Whilst labourers could milk the cows, tend the sheep and, with a simple binder, harvest the corn, milking parlours can only milk and combine harvesters can only harvest cereals. The specialization was made possible by cheap artificial fertilizers, which replaced natural manure, and chemical sprays were developed that allowed the pest control benefits of rotations to be forgone. The application of both fertilizers and chemical sprays was by way of subsidized machinery.

This specialization in turn meant that hedges served little purpose, and the larger machinery that capital subsidies and larger throughputs had induced demanded larger fields; since hedges cost farmers next to nothing to remove, out they came; and footpaths were ploughed over rather than around. This was all greatly exacerbated by the effects of high subsidies on the system as a whole. Higher guaranteed prices, and lower costs, led to higher profits and incomes for farmers. Or would have done, except that they were largely capitalized into land prices. From 1945–7 to 1977–9 these rose in real terms by a factor of 3.5; farmers' incomes, again in real terms, little more than doubled and those of agricultural workers less than doubled.

Thus, the effect of subsidies was not only to increase farm incomes but also to increase the real cost of one factor of production: land, relative to labour and, even more markedly, relative to subsidized capital inputs. The real price of these was falling in any case even without the subsidy. The response of farmers was one an economist would expect: they intensified their use of the now more expensive factor, land. It became more expensive, relatively speaking, to leave land in unproductive use, in hedgerows or footpaths, for example. Generally, it placed further financial pressures on farmers to use their land as intensively as possible to produce subsidized cereals with consequent damage to the rural environment, destruction of the countryside and increased conflict in its use.

This process is not one of the individual farmer changing his spots; or of changing overnight from a conservation-minded traditional mixed farmer, say, to a specialist, heavily capitalized cereal grower who maximizes output regardless of the environmental consequences. Adjustment is primarily of two kinds: relatively small changes year by year of a farmer pushed by the financial pressures and inducements exerted by policy; and quite radical changes in agricultural practices at points when management changes. We found this evident in the study of West Berkshire reported in Chapter 3. In one case a large, traditional, mixed farm was sold and transformed within a matter of two years into an intensive unit, still with both livestock and cereals but with a higher degree of specialization and much greater intensification. In the process nearly all the remaining meadows were ploughed and 60 acres of overgrown copse, very rich in wild life, were uprooted. In addition, access, which had been informal and casual, became firmly limited. In another, the changes accompanied a change of tenancies and the unification of management under one, new, 'scientific' tenant.

Thus there is a yet further way in which the subsidy system has brought about these changes in the countryside. By providing high incomes and strong growth in capital values it has encouraged new types of owners and managers to emerge. It is estimated that financial institutions now own a total of 750,000 acres.[3] As Newby and his associates showed,[4] attitudes to conservation vary systematically between farmers. Traditional family farmers and 'gentleman' farmers are the most sympathetic; paid managers and agribusinessmen, the least. Both the subsidy system (because it tended to squeeze out farmers sympathetic to conservation when land changed management, as they could not afford the new rents or prices) and the subsidy level (because it attracted in a new breed of farmer) brought about a longer term process of transfer of management to those prepared to dance with more enthusiasm to the financial strains devised by policymakers and politicians. Not all responsibility of course lies with bureaucrats. Not only was the National Farmers' Union the only representative industrial body that statutorily had to be consulted by government in the formation of industrial policy; it was also an untiring, well-financed and effective pressure group.

How has this level of support come about? How have we allowed a situation to develop in which agriculture has become totally a creature of state protection, enjoying, as numerous writers have demonstrated,[5] a level of support many times that available to any other industry and far, far beyond that accorded British Steel or British Rail? How has it arisen that the real value of subsidies to agriculture now probably exceeds farmers' net income? At the same time such mountains of surplus production are accumulated that we export butter at a quarter the price at which it is available to European consumers to erode the butter mountain, and sell dried milk off cheap to animal-feed compounders to produce feed for cows to add yet further to the surplus milk (presumably to be dried and fed to cows etc.).

At different times and in different places different arguments have been used. Indeed the impression might be gained that the farming industry and its attendant lobby used whatever arguments they thought would appeal to the fashionable political concern of the time. Immediately after the Second World War the memories of the agricultural depression of the 1920s and 1930s and the wartime shortages were the most important. We had to ensure a fair income for farmers as we tried to build a fairer society and we had to encourage home production for strategic reasons. As we show in Chapters 4 and 7, both these arguments are now clearly irrelevant. Far from being poor, the average farmer in England and Wales, and to a lesser extent Scotland, is now rather rich; at one extreme, we are literally creating millionaires from state subsidies; at another, there are still, particularly in the uplands, quite a number of poor small farmers whose incomes the system has done little for because they can only produce little. Since the bigger and richer the farmer is, the more he gets from the public purse, the present situation is indefensible. As we argue in the final chapter, there is, if you accept the social arguments, a case for an income supplement either to all small/poor farmers or to farmers in the less favoured areas. But there is no case at all for handouts *pro rata* with output that systematically favour the least deserving on grounds of fairness, increase the environmental costs of agriculture and add yet further to the costly mountains of CAP.

The strategic argument has long since been rendered obsolete by the technology of war. We will all go together when we go: farmers, livestock, taxpayers and consumers. Sitting out a prolonged U-boat siege not only can be discounted but, as we can see from the experience of 1940, would be unlikely to be fatal anyway. If we adapted our agriculture and ate less meat, we could even emerge healthier, if less comfortable. But the prospect, in any case, is not a real one.

The arguments of the 1950s and 1960s in favour of agricultural support revolved around the industry's claimed efficiency and the ever-present balance of payments problems Britain experienced. As we show in Chapter 6, claims for agriculture's efficiency were at best based on a confusion (more usually they were part of the agricultural lobby's special pleading). The confusion is between technical and economic efficiency. Naturally, with the subsidies on capital and subsidy-induced high land prices, both output per worker and per unit area increased; especially if you measured output at subsidized, not world, market prices. But the real return on resources used in farming, from the viewpoint of the community as a whole, remained as low as ever. In Britain we could get about twice the output per unit area achieved in North America. That technical efficiency was the result of great capitalization and high subsidized output prices. The capital could have been put into other industries where the return on it would have been much higher than in agriculture. Without the subsidies, farmers could not have afforded their capital spending; and rightly so, since investment in agriculture has not been an efficient use of scarce investment funds. The supply of such funds is not unlimited and so, if more is devoted to agriculture, then less is available to other sectors of the economy. The problems of under-capitalized British industry today are partly the heritage of diverting funds to agricultural investment in the past.

The unreality of the claims for agriculture's efficiency is revealed by the fact that they are used to press for more subsidy. An efficient industry would be able to compete in world terms without subsidy; certainly it would not require subsidy on the scale presently going to farming.

The balance of payments argument was that we should subsidize agriculture to reduce imports of food. This argument is now irrelevant in economic terms because of the removal of the balance of payments constraints as a result of the development of flexible exchange rates and the discovery of North Sea oil. The argument was never valid, however, since it usually ignored the imports that would be induced by agricultural expansion and the exports that would be lost, and always ignored the alternatives available. Imports might be saved by agricultural expansion but so would they by expansion of many other sectors; for example electrical engineering or consumer durables. Since returns from investment were lower in agriculture than manufacturing there was a very strong *a priori* case for believing that more net saving could be achieved by expansion of a whole range of other sectors.

Most recently the agricultural lobby has championed support measures to reduce our net contributions to the Common Agricultural Policy funds. Since CAP is partly funded by taxes on imported food covered by the policy, that is, nearly all products produced on a commercial scale in the EEC, Britain, as a significant net importer, tends to pay a disproportionate share of the cost of CAP. Countries with significant surplus production, most notably Denmark, France and Ireland, tend to receive more through CAP than they contribute. It is our disproportionate budgetary contributions, resulting from the structure of CAP, that have led to continuing efforts by both Labour and Conservative govern-ments to re-negotiate our terms of entry. It is this that has led to the present lack of enthusiasm for British membership in Europe. And it is a related problem – that, as an agricultural surplus country, Spain, too, would share in the spoils of CAP – that underlies French objections to Spanish entry.

The agricultural lobby in Britain argues that by national measures to give yet more support to agriculture, we can, by expanding domestic output, reduce our contribution to the EEC budget. This argument is dealt with fully in Chapter 7. It depends on expanding production of items where, in many cases, additional output, once you allow for support measures, actually reduces rather than increases the real value of national income. This is already true (see Chapter 5) for milk production. It does not, of course, follow that we should produce no milk in the UK. There is little doubt that even with no support at all the great bulk of liquid milk consumption would be home produced – and some milk for manufacturing too. But, since entry to the EEC, milk for manufacturing has increased by 75 per cent whilst liquid consumption has declined. Expansion of farm output would also, apart from its costs in priced resources, have a real resource cost in terms of a yet further detrimental impact on the countryside.

In a rich and leisured society, where obesity is a greater health risk than malnutrition – despite unemployment and slow growth this is still the case in Europe in the 1980s – it is absurd to pretend that adding to surplus food production gives a clear economic benefit; whilst environmental quality, pure water supplies, pollution or beautiful countryside, are figments of some namby-pamby environmentalist's imagination. Such intangible goods and bads contribute to overall economic welfare in ways just as important as additional cream, dried milk or veal production. The problem is just that markets attach no prices to them and policy does not make good that deficiency.

It seems to us that in the context of continuing membership of the EEC, very much the most positive policy for British agriculture and the countryside is to reform the CAP radically and drastically lower the overall level of European farm subsidies. Pressures for such changes are developing in Europe quite independently of any efforts Britain might make. There is a problem of endemic surplus which the high support levels make ever worse. To this has recently been added the efforts of Greek farmers and it appears soon will be added the surpluses of Spain. The European budget goes from financial crisis to financial crisis. Reform cannot be far away.

The logical policy for Britain, but also for the rest of Europe and the rest of the world, is to aim to stabilize prices farmers receive at little above the average world market price whilst allowing consumers to buy food at world market prices. In short, to adopt for Europe a form of the British 1950's system of deficiency payments, but at a lower level of average protection and without capital subsidies (they could form part of individual member states' national policies if required). In purely short-term national terms Denmark, France or Ireland, as the largest exporters, would be the prime losers, though their non-agricultural population would gain from lower food prices and less pressure on the environment. If lower food prices fed through to lower inflation and lower investment in agriculture to foster growth, all sections of Danish, French and Irish society would benefit in the medium term. How the CAP penalizes non-EEC countries is discussed in Chapter 5.

To these subsidies could be added (i) income supplements for small farmers in the 'less favoured areas' if it was thought socially desirable (though it would be imperative that they were so designed that their value did not merely become capitalized in the land values of small farms); and (ii) amenity subsidies to reward farmers for their contribution to social welfare where they adopt farming practices in harmony with the rural environment and/or that enhance the production of unpriced social value created by an accessible and attractive countryside.

Some, for example Marion Shoard,[6] have argued that the means by which the countryside should be safeguarded, and the community's interest secured, is the extension of existing planning controls to cover the countryside and features such as permanent pasture or hedgerows within it. This proposal is, we believe, misguided. It would, if agricultural policy continued as at present, create a situation where one branch of government was spending more than a thousand million pounds a year,[7] and providing additional price support usually worth more thousands of millions, to bring about changes that a far weaker arm of government, with no financial leverage, was attempting, via controls, to prevent. The first step towards protecting the rural environment is to reduce the level of agricultural subsidies. By so doing the apparent need for controls will become much weaker and largely disappear. In addition, if planning controls were to have a significant impact on the environment the costs of administration would be immense. We now charge for planning applications. Past experience would lead one to expect that planning applications in agriculture would be grant-aided! The experience of listed building control demonstrates the difficulty of preserving through controls where the financial incentives are to destroy. The solution, then, is to eliminate the incentives to destroy and introduce incentives to conserve.

Since we first advocated amenity subsidies in 1969,[8] they have been introduced. The most recent context is the Wildlife and Countryside Act 1981 which provides for them in the case of refusal of grant aid for damaging Sites of Special Scientific Interest (SSSI). The fundamental problem with significant use of amenity subsidies, at present, is their cost.

The problem arises because of the absurd system of calculation. This point is discussed in detail in Chapter 8. The system for protecting SSSIs follows broadly the principles established in the voluntary scheme to protect moorland on Exmoor. The cost of preventing farmers from ploughing one of the few remaining areas of chalk downland or draining a wetland meadow, will include not only the value of the subsidy forgone but also the capitalized value of all subsidies that would have been received on food that will not be produced, and which in any case we don't want. Part of this problem disappears if, as we suggest, grant aid is drastically reduced. But there is a continuing problem of amenity subsidies in a heavily supported agricultural system. Given that most farm net income comes by one route or another from support, compensation for income forgone is inevitably mainly compensation for loss of that support. Since the bulk of support is through high consumer prices maintained via the CAP, one result of using amenity subsidies to prevent the destruction of countryside features would be to transfer the burden of support from citizens as consumers to citizens as taxpayers. But the increase in public expenditure (the amenity subsidy) is an over-statement of the cost to society of countryside protection. The real cost of that is given by valuing the agricultural outputs and inputs at world market prices. As we point out later, this will be much less than the cost of compensation[9] and in some cases, where the true value of output is less than its true production costs, will be negative!

So in paying compensation within the present system of agricultural protection, conservation is taking over a part of the burden of agricultural support. The answer is simplicity itself. The conservation accounts should pay only that proportion of any amenity subsidy that represents a true cost of conservation; MAFF and European agricultural funds should pay what in most cases will be far the larger proportion, the true costs of agricultural support. Saddling amenity subsidies with the costs of agricultural support as at present means that they become impossibly expensive. We have the absurd situation that farmers must be offered large sums of money as inducements *not to* plough up rare habitats or expanses of open moorland because they are simultaneously being offered large sums as inducements *to* plough.

Conservationists are often told they should face the economic facts of life. Part of the purpose of this book is to show that it is rather farmers who should face economic facts. At present, as the story of oilseed rape so graphically illustrates, they operate in a hothouse world constructed by policymakers where costs and prices bear no relation either to true resource costs or community preferences. The private financial facts that this world has created for farmers – their costs of production and farm gate prices – are foisted on a long-suffering public. There is a powerful case for the community to shape these facts so that it pays farmers not only to produce food but to produce the sort of countryside that the community enjoys.

This would require above all a lower level of subsidy on average and the abolition of capital grants. In an era of unemployment, labour grants would make more sense. But whilst people willingly pay farmers through the market to produce food, they do not pay them to produce pleasant countryside. Unlike the former, the latter cannot be imported. If we are going to pay farmers anything other than what they can earn, we should pay them for keeping amenities, not for destroying them.

Notes

1 Cheshire, P. C. and Bowers, J. K. (1969) 'Farming conservation and amenity', *New Scientist*, 3 April.
2 Shoard, M. (1980) *The Theft of the Countryside*, London, Temple Smith.
3 Steel, A. and Byrne, P. J. (1983) 'Financial institutions: their investments and agricultural landownership'. University of Reading, Department of Land Management Working Paper no. 1.

4 Newby, H., Bell, C. and Rose, D. (1977) 'Farmers' attitudes to conservation', *Countryside Recreation Review*, vol. 2.
5 See for example, McCrone, G. (1962) *The Economics of Subsidising Agriculture*, London; Allen & Unwin, Food and Agriculture Organization of the United Nations (1973), *Agricultural Protection: Domestic Policy and International Trade* C 73/LIM/9; Corbett, H. and Niall, J. (1976) 'Strategy for the liberalisation of agricultural trade', in Davey, B., Josling, T. E. and McFarquhar, A. (eds) *Agriculture and the State*, London, Macmillan; Black, C. J. and Bowers, J. K. (1981) 'The level of protection of U.K. agriculture', University of Leeds, School of Economic Studies Discussion Paper no. 99.
6 Shoard (1980), op. cit.
7 The Public Expenditure White Paper for 1983–4 to 1984–5 (Cmnd 8789 – I and II) estimates direct government spending on agricultural support in 1982/3 at £1660 million.
8 Cheshire and Bowers (1969), op. cit.
9 For an example of what difference it makes see *New Scientist*, 10 February 1983, p. 357.

2

Agriculture and the countryside

In the post-war period there has been a very rapid increase in the use made of the British countryside by the urban population. The uses made of the countryside are many and varied, but almost all activities – rural-based recreational pursuits in the planners' jargon – have been on a rising trend. Walking in the countryside, with over 8 million participants, is now the most popular sport in England and Wales.[1]

The extent of this increase is a little difficult to document since no fully comprehensive national data on the ways in which people spend their leisure time have been collected. It is reflected in the membership of societies concerned with recreational activities. Thus between 1960 and 1980 The Ramblers' Association tripled its membership and the British Horse Society increased its membership by a factor of $4\frac{1}{2}$ from 1960 to 1978. Overnight stays at YHA hostels almost doubled between 1960 and 1978.[1] Similarly membership of organizations concerned with natural history pursuits, the Royal Society for the Protection of Birds and the County Natural History Societies and Naturalist Trusts, have had growing membership. The growth of the traditional rural exploitive activities, hunting and shooting, has been less marked, with the exception of fishing which has become a very popular urban working-class pursuit and in 1980 had 1.2 million adherents.[1]

But these more purposive uses of the countryside are only part of the story. The most marked change has been the growth of more casual visits to the countryside to walk, picnic or just sit. The extent of such activities has been determined in a number of surveys. From these it appears that about three-quarters of the urban population participate in at least one day trip to the countryside during the year. A study for the southeast of England suggested that a third of the population participated in 'countryside open space activities' on more than 20 occasions during the year. That these activities are growing is indicated by traffic censuses and by visitor counts in National Parks and other designated areas that have been monitored. The volume of summer weekend traffic in national parks and other rural areas increased by an average of about 35 per cent over the period 1966–73. Over the period 1963–70, visitors to the Peak District National Park more than doubled.

Recreational use of the countryside is, of course, not confined to day visitors. In the New Forest camping increased at an annual rate of 14 per cent from 1957 with higher rates in the late 1960s.[2] In 1970 no fewer than 4 million people went camping and the National Caravan Council estimated that by 1974 there were 360,000 touring caravans in use.

The main factors leading to this growth of use of the countryside appear to be increased mobility arising from the growth in ownership of the private motor car, which is the form of transport for the vast majority of visits to the countryside, and increasing incomes and leisure. The growth of demand has probably been sustained by changes in tastes for leisure activities – evidenced by the much slower growth of visits to the traditional seaside resorts and the decline in demand for holiday camps. In addition, however, it is clear that as people get richer their demand for amenity use of the countryside increases; in technical terms the income elasticity of demand for countryside pursuits is positive and may be greater than unity: that is, as people get richer, they devote an increasing proportion of their income to such pursuits. The growth in popularity of the countryside is observable for all age groups and income levels. The trend looks set to continue. The Department of the Environment predicts an increase in the number of holiday and day trips to rural areas of 50 per cent between 1972 and 1990.

Given that 85 per cent of the non-urban land surface of the
United Kingdom is under some form of agriculture, excluding
forestry and woodlands,[3] the supply of facilities to meet this
recreational demand and the growth of it must come from
agricultural land. In technical terms agricultural output and
recreational facilities broadly defined are joint products; that is
they are supplied together by the same activities of the farmer. In
the formulation of agricultural policy[4] no account has been taken
of the requirements of other users of agricultural land and indeed
for much of the post-war period the nature of recreation as a
product jointly supplied with agriculture was not even recognized. If anything, other demands on agricultural land have been
regarded as nuisances that interfere with efficient agricultural
practice and losses of amenity resulting from changing agricultural practice continue to be treated as of small moment and
something that the urban population must bear for the greater
good of increasing agricultural production and productivity. This
attitude is not based on any formal evaluation of the relative
values of the joint products. Rather it results from the narrow
perspective of the Ministry of Agriculture. It has, with some
justice, been called a 'Ministry for Farmers', although it could be
contended that the Ministry policy has not been in the best
interest of farmers either.[5] While one might say that there are some
straws in the wind – the Ministry has belatedly recognized its
responsibility to the consumers of foodstuffs – the 'amenity as
nuisance' view still permeates official thinking. It is visible in the
1975 White Paper *Food From Our Own Resources*,[6] which blandly
asserts, in the teeth of overwhelming evidence to the contrary,
that the proposed expansion programme 'should not result in any
undesirable changes in the environment'.[7] It is visible also in the
Countryside Review Committee's Discussion paper *Food Production in the Countryside* which, after arguing that 'for the first time
in our history there is an increasing divergence between farming
on the one hand and landscape and nature conservation on the
other', concludes that nothing can be done about this, except in
the uplands where 'agricultural justification for farming is weaker
than in other areas'.[8]

We profoundly disagree with this view. Even in the agricultural
heartlands, the lowlands, the economic case for intensive agriculture and even more the case for increasing intensification of

agriculture is extremely weak. The value of food produced at the margin on even the best land is below its cost of production. The urban population foots the bill for this inefficient use of resources and suffers at the same time the denial of its legitimate demands on the countryside and the concomitant destruction of the environment. This argument is developed in succeeding chapters. For the present we consider the extent and nature of the conflict.

At the same time that the demand of the urban population for amenity use of the countryside has increased, trends in agricultural practice, under the spur of agricultural policy, have reduced the value of the countryside for these uses and agricultural production and amenity use have come increasingly into conflict. The direction of agricultural change has been towards increasing intensity of land use and specialization of production with increasing intensity in the use of chemical inputs and machinery. The ways in which these trends have damaged the interests of other users of the countryside may be analysed under a number of heads.

First, and most obviously, there has been a reduction in access to agricultural land. This has not taken, for the most part, the form of legal closure of footpaths. Indeed the area devoted to footpaths has not been reduced very much and has in part been compensated for by the co-ordination of footpath routes and the creation of long-distance footpaths. It is worth noting, however, that the lowest densities of footpaths are in counties with high proportions of intensive arable farming, notably in the Fens, and places like Hampshire, Berkshire and Oxfordshire with large corn-growing areas.[9] Much more important has been the illegal closure and diversion of footpaths, the great increase in ploughing and the failure to restore footpaths after ploughing. Few walkers are willing to trudge across ploughland, even though they have a legal right to do so. Even fewer are willing to plunge into the middle of a field of corn. This has meant that the mere act of ploughing up and planting a footpath is often *de facto* sufficient to close it, despite legal safeguards. The problem has been compounded by hedgerow removal since there is a tendency for footpaths to follow hedgerows and field boundaries. The elimination of these hedgerows and the alteration of field boundaries opens the way for *de facto* closure by ploughing and/or planting.

But the really significant change has been the reduction in access away from footpaths. There are two aspects of this.

First, the extent of unused or underused field margins, or other odd corners of scrub, where public access created no damage to agricultural interest has been drastically reduced, particularly in the lowlands. The best index of this loss is the rate of hedgerow removal. The Countryside Commission[10] estimated that the rate of hedgerow removal 'rose to a peak in the mid 1960s with a loss of about 10,000 miles per year. This rate of loss has been substantially reduced since 1970, but removal continues in many parts of the country. In some eastern counties more than half the hedgerows were lost in the 25 years up to 1972.' Similarly, 'up to 80 per cent of the trees have been lost in the last 25 years in some arable counties in the east of England'. The Commission also noted that many small woodlands had been cleared and reclaimed for agriculture over the same period, although they were unable to supply statistics on this aspect of the problem.

Second, those forms of agriculture which are most compatible with recreational use of the land have declined. Apart from rough shooting on stubble, virtually no recreational activity is compatible with arable farming. One must look, therefore, to land under grass. Over the period 1953–73 the acreage designated in the agricultural censuses as permanent grass declined by 12 per cent and that as rough grazings by almost 13 per cent.[11] Over the same period the total agricultural acreage decreased by under 5 per cent. This decline was not uniform over the country. For example, the decline in permanent grass was 3 per cent in Derbyshire and 42 per cent in Bedfordshire. What has happened is best shown by expressing the figures in another form.

Over the same 20-year period the proportion of total agricultural acreage of England that was under either permanent grass or rough grazings fell by four percentage points – from 49 per cent to 45 per cent. Falls were greater than this in counties where the area of grass was low (see Table 2.1), and in counties with or close to large urban areas where the demand for recreational use could be expected to be high (see Table 2.2). The declines were much less marked in the areas in the west and north where the national parks were located. There was a rise of one percentage point in Derbyshire and no change in Wales, although in both cases there was a switch from rough grazing to permanent grass which implied a reduction in accessibility and a rise in potential conflict.

The consequence of these trends in agricultural practices has been to render large tracts of the countryside difficult of access

Table 2.1   Decline of permanent grass

county	% under grass		change (% points)
	1953	1973	
Norfolk	22	16	6
Cambridge and Ely	14	9	5
Essex	22	16	6
Bedfordshire	27	17	10

Source: MAFF Agricultural Statistics: England and Wales, annual.

and unsuitable for recreational use. Furthermore, these changes have created a landscape which most people do not find attractive.[12] Where access is possible it is largely not desired. That these changes have occurred most strongly in areas where the demand for recreational use of the countryside, because of population pressure or deficiency of suitable supply, has been greatest, has aggravated the problem. Inevitably it has concentrated the pressure on the areas that remain suitable, increasing the problems for nature reserves, national parks and similar areas.

Another way of explaining the geographic pattern observed is to say that the trends towards increasing agricultural intensity are most in evidence in the lowlands and on the chalk and limestone.

Table 2.2   Decline of permanent grass

county	% under grass		change (% points)
	1953	1973	
Berkshire	35	26	9
Oxfordshire	40	31	9
Buckinghamshire	51	44	7
Leicestershire	52	43	9
Nottinghamshire	33	23	10
Gloucestershire	52	47	5

Source: MAFF Agricultural Statistics: England and Wales, annual.

However they are spreading to uplands where land drainage and pasture improvement have been at a high rate over the last few years.

The second consequence of changing agricultural practices has been a sharp reduction in the diversity of habitat with consequent destruction of plant and animal communities. This aspect of the problem has been the subject of an authoritative study by the Nature Conservancy Council (NCC).[13] The following paragraphs do no more than précis the conclusions and report some of the findings of that study.

The reduction in diversity of habitat derives from a number of facets of modern agricultural practice.

(i)   the removal of hedgerows and the ploughing up of un-cultivated field margins together with the reclamation of scrub and small woodlands;
(ii) the reduction in rotations and fallows;
(iii) the replacement of permanent pasture by leys and arable;
(iv) land drainage and the elimination of areas of standing water and farm ponds;
(v)   the treatment of grassland and arable with selective herbicides and insecticides.

The consequences for wildlife have been an undoubted disaster. An indication is given by a comparison between un-modernized farms with hedges and semi-natural grass verges and modernized farms with wire fences and sown grass. Some 20 species of mammals, 37 species of birds and 17 species of butterflies may be found in the former. In the latter the equivalent numbers are 5, 6 and zero. Similarly some 20 species of butterflies may be found on untreated permanent pasture in which the food plants for their larvae grow. None can exist on grass leys. The elimination of permanent ponds and ditches and their replacement by temporary ditches and piped water entails similar reductions in the diversity of habitats and species. As a result the NCC calculates that:

> If all farms were totally modernised so that they consisted solely of arable crops, grass leys, chemically treated ditches, farm buildings and a few trees and bushes grown for visual amenity . . . about 80% of the bird and about 95% of the butterfly species would be lost from the farmed landscape.[17]

It is already clear that there have been serious declines in a number of plant and animal species but the extent of these declines is difficult to quantify. The best way of doing this is to consider the number of 10-km squares in which a species occurs. The Nature Conservancy Council give an example of a rare butterfly, the silver-spotted skipper, which has vanished from 69 per cent of the squares in which it had been found before 1960. Of dragonfly species which occurred in fewer than 200 squares in Great Britain, excluding migratory species, those confined to North Scotland, and three which are apparently extinct, the squares with post-1960 records are on average 40 per cent fewer. The percentage reduction rises to an average of 45 per cent if one considers those occurring in fewer than 100 squares and to 50 per cent for those recorded in fewer than 50 squares.[14] For other insects, for amphibia, mammals and birds, the information is not in a usable form or is still being collected.

The best data are for plants. Here we can do no better than again to quote the Nature Conservancy Council study referred to. Defining rare plants as those which occurred in fewer than 15 10-km squares in 1930, it was found that there had been a 30 per cent loss by 1960. As with dragonflies this loss was greatest in the very rare species. In 1900, 44 species occurred in one or two squares only. This number had risen to 97 species by 1970. Twenty other species which had occurred in more than 20 squares in 1900 were reduced to fewer than 10 squares by 1970. An examination of the probable source of extinction and declines of rarer British plants since 1800 suggested that 50 per cent was due to changes in agriculture and drainage and only 26 per cent to natural 'causes' and 7 per cent to habitat destruction by building and other causes. The Conservancy noted that 'parallel reductions have occurred in the population of many common species'.

As modern agriculture has impoverished the environment so the importance of the remaining still rich habitats, a small proportion of them classified as nature reserves, has increased. Agriculture has created the need for nature reserves by a wholesale destruction of the environment as at the same time, by restricting accessibility as described, it has increased the pressure on them. The major threat to the environment comes not from population pressure and increased urbanization, nor from that coupled with increased personal mobility and wealth, but from changing agricultural techniques.

One final point is in order. The official Scheduled Sites of Special Scientific Interest scheduled under the Countryside Act of 1949 and under the charge of the Nature Conservancy, which are given protection from urban development, have also suffered from the trends in agriculture. Change in agricultural use does not constitute a change in land use under the various planning acts and considerable numbers have been destroyed or damaged despite being scheduled. The Conservancy now has the power to enter into agreements with the landowner for the protection of these sites and the situation, as is discussed in Chapter 8, has been improved by the Wildlife Act 1981. But the rate of loss is still considerable.

There have also been broader environmental consequences of intensive agriculture arising from its use of chemicals. These are what economists call external diseconomies of the system. One of the best documented of these effects is the build up of organochlorine residues in birds of prey. These resulted in serious reductions in breeding success and consequently in the population levels of many birds of prey, particularly the larger and rarer species. Recovery has only been partial despite restrictions on the use of the pesticides concerned.

Algae blooms in lakes and ponds from fertilizer run-off is another example. This appears to have led to the extinction of one dragonfly species, *Coenagrian armatum*, and possibly a second, *Lestes dryas*. It is probably an additional cause of decline in aquatic fauna and is a factor in the ecological deterioration of the Norfolk Broads. The extent and form of ecological changes induced by agricultural chemicals are largely unknown since chemical ecology is yet in its infancy.

Chemical run-off from agriculture is also a cause of the pollution of water supplies. An article in *The Sunday Times*[15] reported that over a hundred important sources of public water supply are now so contaminated with nitrates that they cannot be used directly and that some wells have had to be shut down completely. Furthermore, research by the Water Research Centre reveals that there are vast quantities of nitrates slowly percolating down towards the country's main aquifers and predicts that in 10–20 years underground supplies, accounting for about 30 per cent of the country's water needs, could have nitrate concentrations above the WHO warning level. While there is no simple relationship between fertilizer use and nitrate concentrations, it is clear that intensive agriculture is a major course of nitrate pollution in underground water supplies: the rise in the problem is closely correlated with the trend in fertilizer use and the geographical distribution of the problem is related to intensive arable farming. Furthermore, the Water Research team have developed a model which enables them to predict underground nitrate concentrations from land use patterns.

In addition to these consequences, there are high costs of sewage disposal from intensive livestock rearing with the additional resource costs of substituting for nitrogen in the specialist arable areas. Furthermore, those concerned with the preservation of fossil fuels should note that intensive agriculture is a heavy user, directly and indirectly, of these exhaustible resources. Nor should it be thought that developments in agriculture have increased the economy's independence from the rest of the world. Increasing specialization has meant increasing dependence on imports, for animal feeds, chemicals, oils and machinery.

As well as being detrimental to the interests of the general user of the countryside, the naturalist and the ecologist, modern developments have brought agriculture into conflict with the historian and the archaeologist. In 1964 the then Ministry of Public Buildings and Works carried out a survey of ancient monuments scheduled under the Ancient Monuments Act and charged to its care in Wiltshire, a county particularly rich in them. Of 640 ancient monuments scheduled in the county at the time, 250 were found to have been destroyed or seriously damaged and 150 less badly damaged. Almost all of this damage was the result of agricultural practice, largely ploughing; it had all taken place over the previous 10 years. Damage on this scale was shown to have taken place in other parts of the country. Other evidence also points in the same direction. Thus the 13th Annual Report of the Deserted Medieval Village (DMV) Research Group,[16] summarized the position of DMV sites in the country. Of 2000 DMVs identified at that date some 246 were destroyed before 1939 (perhaps centuries before); a further 36 sites were destroyed by ploughing between 1939 and 1952; between 1952 and 1965 a further 201 were destroyed or were threatened with destruction. Thus the report comments 'it will be seen that as many sites have been threatened during the past 25 years as during the previous 500 years'.

Finally it is necessary to mention that not all of the damage from increasing agricultural intensity is directly attributable to the activities of farmers. A major and increasing threat to the surviving wetlands of lowland Britain stems from the activities of the drainage divisions of the Regional Water Authorities constituted under the Water Act 1973 and given additional functions by the Land Drainage Act of 1976. By the early 1970s most of the marshland areas in river valleys, in lowland England at least, that could be drained by farmers without prior arterial drainage work by the water authorities *had* been drained. The drainage divisions of the WAs – and the River Boards that preceded them – have seen their function as the elimination of all risk of flooding to agricultural land and all wetland habitats within their areas. To this end they have straightened and widened streams and rivers under their control, removing river vegetation and cutting down riverside trees that interfered with the efficiency of water-courses as drains and the free movement of their mechanical diggers. At the instigation of the Internal Drainage Boards – basically committees of farmers who pay drainage rates – which have performed the same activities for water courses and ditches off of main rivers – they have raised embankments and installed pumping schemes so as to facilitate field drainage by farmers. Their role here has not been merely permissive, providing the necessary improvements in arterial drainage when the landowners and occupiers have requested, rather they have seen themselves as missionaries and propagandists for the virtues of land drainage. Thus in a recent report the Wessex Water Authority comments that:

> *the River Authority has tended to pioneer the way* and has accepted that the take-up by farmers of the benefits of improved drainage may be over a prolonged period. This is not unusual with innovations. *It requires the courage of the first few* to prove a belief before the majority will join in and take advantage of the benefits (our italics).[18]

Despite the lukewarm response by the farmers affected, the authority states firmly its 'intention . . . to continue to implement capital schemes to improve drainage to enable the agricultural potential of the area to be achieved'.[19]

The water authority has a statutory obligation to consider the effects of its activities on fauna and flora. We consider its activities are plainly detrimental to these. The report we are quoting states:

> with increasing interest and pressure from conservationists it must be manifestly apparent that any drainage schemes it promotes are requested and supported by the farming community[20]

and yet the authority continues to sell drainage to the farmers.

The extent of this activity by the water authorities can be gauged from the same report. For the Somerset Local Land Drainage District alone some 500 'problems' of flooding of agricultural land are identified and solutions involving expenditure to improve the drainage suggested.

But more worrying than the minor works over recent years has been the willingness of the water authorities to instigate major schemes for the drainage and reclamation of large wetland areas.

In 1979 a scheme by the Southern Water Authority to permit, by raising the river embankment and installing a pumping station, the reclamation of 200 hectares of marshland, mainly SSSI, along the River Arun at Amberley Wildbrooks in Sussex, was defeated at a public inquiry; but this was only after the Southern Water Authority had, without any effective protest, caused the drainage of most of the other wetland areas in the Arun valley.

But this scheme was only small beer in comparison with other schemes in existence. The Anglian Water Authority has a proposal, with which it is determined to proceed, for a barrier on the Yare at Great Yarmouth. On their assessment[21] this scheme should lead over a 20-year period to the conversion of 8000 hectares of marshland in the Yare, Bure and Waveney valleys, i.e. all the valleys of the Norfolk Broads, to arable and intensive grassland. A scheme of similar magnitude is under consideration for the River Parrett in Somerset. In conjunction with major works on the River Bure this should lead to the elimination of all problems of flooding and drainage, i.e. all wetlands in the Sedgemoor Levels. Smaller schemes – smaller because the wetlands concerned are smaller in area – exist for the Idle Washes in the Trent catchment area and the Derwent Valley in Yorkshire, and there are doubtless others of which we are unaware. These schemes extend the possibilities of intensive farming, heighten the environmental damage that it causes, and exacerbate the conflict, already severe enough, between farming and other uses of the countryside.

It should be added that the damage of agriculture is being extended also to the coastal environment, by the direct reclamation for agricultural purposes of salt marsh. There has been an acceleration in the rate of reclamation of the Wash saltings – virtually all classified as SSSI – to the point where very little mature salting of high ecological value remains. A major scheme of reclamation on the Ribble estuary, again for agricultural purposes, in 1979 was only prevented after a long battle and at great public expense.

In conclusion it can be seen that modern trends in agriculture have damaged and threatened the interests of all users of the countryside, the specialist and the generalist. Modern agriculture is incompatible with almost everything else. The reasons for these developments and an economic appraisal of them is the subject of the rest of this book. They are not the result of inexorable economic forces about which nothing can be done. They are the consequences of agricultural policy consciously pursued with a high level of protection and paid for directly and indirectly by the taxpayer and the consumer of foodstuffs; largely, in fact, by the urban user of the countryside whose interests they threaten and who has virtually no say in their course.

Notes

1 Probably the most convenient and up-to-date surveys of recreational activities are: The Countryside Commission (1979), *Digest of Countryside Recreation Statistics 1979* and The Sports Council (1983) *A Digest of Sports Statistics*, 1st edn, Information Series no. 7. These are the source of the data used here.
2 Forestry Commission, Hampshire County Council, Nature Conservancy Council and others (1970) *Conservation of the New Forest*, joint report. Lyndhurst, Hampshire.
3 See Best, R. H. (1981) *Land Use and Living Space*, London, Methuen, Table 8.
4 As opposed to forestry policy. We are considering agriculture as a separate industry from forestry.
5 Really it has been in the interests of 'farming' as an abstract entity existing in the mind of the Ministry.

6   *Food From Our Own Resources* (1975) Cmnd 6020, London, HMSO, April.
7   Para. 54. It is under the aegis of this expansion programme, incidentally, that the water authorities have launched some major reclamation schemes which threaten some of the rarest and most valuable wetland habitats (Amberley Wildbrooks, Somerset Levels and Yare Levels).
8   Countryside Review Committee (1977) *Food Production in the Countryside*, Topic Paper no. 2, London, HMSO.
9   See the map in Rucksack (1970) vol. 6, no. 1, winter.
10 Countryside Commission (1977) *New Agricultural Landscapes: Issues, Objectives and Action*, July, London.
11 These figures are derived from MAFF Agricultural Statistics: England and Wales, annual.
12 As the Countryside Review Committee comments laconically: 'In landscape terms we must make a largely qualitative assessment, but general opinion would undoubtedly be that the new is not simply unfamiliar but also inferior' (*Food Production in the Countryside* (1978) Topic Paper no. 3, London, HMSO).
13 Nature Conservancy Council (1977) *Nature Conservation and Agriculture*, March, London.
14 Data culled from Hammond, C. O. (1977) *The Dragonflies of Great Britain and Ireland*, London, Curwen Press.
15 Silcock, B. (1978) 'Where our water fails the health test' *The Sunday Times* 23 July, p. 12.
16 Deserted Medieval Village Research Group (1976) *13th Annual Report*, mimeo, Leeds.
17 Nature Conservancy Council (1977), op. cit., p. 12.
18 Wessex Water Authority, Somerset Local Land Drainage District (1979) *Land Drainage Survey Report*, Bridgewater, Somerset, p. 186.
19 ibid., p. 3.
20 ibid., p. 186.
21 Anglian Water Authority, Norfolk and Suffolk River Division (1977) *Yare Basin Flood Control Study*, vol. 2, final report, Tables 5.2 and 5.5, Norwich.

3

Countryside changes in West Berkshire

The purpose of this chapter is to document in some detail the changes that have occurred (from 1947 to 1981) in a 20 square kilometre area of West Berkshire. The area has been chosen for its ordinariness. Other studies have looked at some of the dramatic changes; at, for example, the conflicts on Exmoor and the loss of outstanding areas of downland. The drainage proposals for areas such as the Norfolk Broads or the Somerset Levels have received considerable publicity. Much material relating to these dramatic changes has been gathered and eloquently summarized by Marion Shoard[1] who likewise has brought together much of the information relating to changes in the countryside nationally. In contrast, the aim of this chapter is to examine the particular and the unexceptional. We wish to document what has happened and show how the changes we discover relate to agricultural change; which in turn, as we argue throughout this book, does not result from some *deus ex machina* of disembodied technical progress but from direct human intervention by policy makers, by ideologically based and, in the main, publicly directed research and, above all, by a hearty slice of public money. The punch line throughout is that the degradation of the countryside and of the rural environment, so widely decried by the urban public, is produced by the subsidies the urban public, all but unknowingly, provide.

In the study area of West Berkshire, as in most of the British Isles within reach of a major conurbation, agricultural change has interacted with the social and economic changes associated with urban decentralization in effecting its transformation of the countryside.

The area which is the focus of this chapter is bounded by grid lines SU 40 and 45 east and 76 and 80 north. It lies on the edge of the Berkshire downs between Newbury and Wantage. Its location is illustrated in Figure 3.1, which also provides a sketch map of the main features of the area as a whole. The eastern and western fringes are chalk downland soils but in the main central part there is a deep clay overlay and the soil, though heavy, is quite rich and deep. As a matter of literary interest, the western fringe of the area formed part of the backdrop to much of Hardy's *Jude the Obscure*,[2] which also provides some description of the area's appearance in the nineteenth century.

The Berkshire downs themselves were, and still are, some of the most sparsely populated areas of lowland England, historically because of the poverty of their soils. The central section of the study area is the tip of a finger running northwards from Newbury of richer soils, denser population and more wooded countryside. Overall at the start of the period nearly 10 per cent of the area was wooded, as Table 3.1 shows. The population is concentrated in three villages, Chaddleworth, Leckhampstead and Brightwalton; the last two villages contain still distinct sub-sections. In Leckhampstead there is Leckhampstead Thicket, the area around the church and Leckhampstead Street, though recent 'in-filling' has merged those latter two areas. In Brightwalton there is the village area around the church, Brightwalton Green and the area around Pudding Lane.

There are two quite substantial country houses set in parkland within the area, Woolley and Chaddleworth Houses. Both are occupied by families who have a long-term local connection. The Woolley estate is the largest single landowner within the area, the land now being farmed primarily by two tenants, one of whom manages a very substantial acreage. There are also a number of other substantial independent farms, such as the Manor farms at Brightwalton and Leckhampstead, Oakash farm and Eastley. There are, in addition, a number of smaller farms such as Malthouse, Purley or Stevens' farms. In the period since 1947

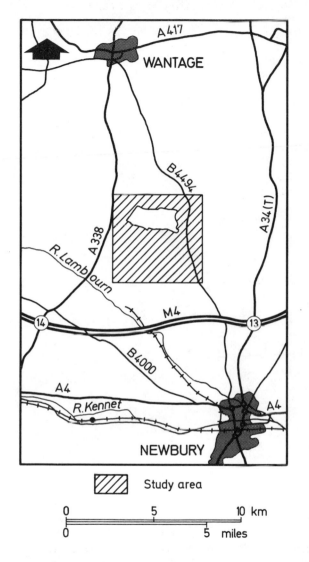

Study area

| 0 | | 5 | | 10 km |
| 0 | | | 5 | miles |

Figure 3.1   Location map of study area

Table 3.1 Countryside changes in an area of West Berkshire, 1947–76, with major changes to 1981

	main study area[1]			area of figure 3.2		
	1947	1976	1981	1947	1976	1981
hedges total						
kms	129.0	83.2	74.1	24.8	16.6	15.2
% change		−35.5	−10.9		−33.1	−8.4
hedges: double trees						
kms	...	...	...	6.3	3.5	3.2
% change		...	...		−44.4	−8.6
hedges and standard trees						
kms	62.3	36.4	33.2	8.7	5.1	2.7
% change		−41.6	−8.8		−41.4	−47.1
hedges: no trees						
kms	66.7	46.8	40.9	9.8	8.0	9.3
% change		−29.8	−12.6		−18.4	+16.3
visible footpaths/tracks						
kms	31.3	15.1	14.4	5.8	3.5	3.1
% change		−51.8	−4.6		−39.7	−11.4
ponds: number	25	9	8	8	1	1
% change		−64.0	−11.1		−87.5	—
working farms: number	19	14	12	4	2	2
% change		−26.3	−14.3		−50.0	—
new agricultural buildings	...	...	...		6	0

				3	2	1
industrial locations with employment	—	—	—			
woodland						
hectares	183.1	170.8	138.2	30.35	30.35	30.35
% change	—	−6.7	−19.1	—	−33.3	−50.0
arable[2]						
hectares	897.7	1246.7	...	146.7	213.9	—
% change	—	+38.9	...	—	+45.8	Some decline
permanent pasture[3]						
hectares	563.5	114.1	...	85.3	5.9	—
% change	—	−79.8	...	—	−93.1	Small increase
ley pasture						
hectares	191.3	262.8	...	24.8	30.0	—
% change	—	−37.4	...	—	+21.0	Some increase
residential area						
hectares	56.3	84.2	—	7.9	13.4	14.0
% change	—	+49.6	—	—	+69.6	+4.5
recreational area						
hectares	2.4	30.2	30.2	—	—	—
% change	—	+1158.3	—	—	—	—

Source: See text.

1 Study area defined in text.

2 Nearly all made up of cereals; remainder in 1947 was mainly brassica crops. In 1976 included substantial area of rape.

3 Includes 36.1 hectares of parkland at both dates. In 1947 included small area of orchard.

. . . Information not available.

— Nil or negligible.

there have been some farm amalgamations, the most significant of which was probably that of Green and Manor farms on the Woolley estate in the mid-1960s.

The primary sources of data were air photographs. By a happy coincidence the area was surveyed in 1947, the watershed year of agricultural policy; a mosaic made from photos taken in September 1947 exists. It was possible to supplement this information with a set of photos taken of most of the area in April 1946, which greatly assisted the identification of permanent pasture in particular. The 1946 survey omits a small section in the south of the area where there is a defence establishment, USAF Welford. The 1947 mosaic fabricated an imaginary landscape for this, so the section intruding into the study area was simply excluded.

The information for 1976 and 1981 was derived from the 1976 air survey and from a ground survey. The 1981 data only adjust for major changes, however, such as the clearance of a large area of ancient woodland and some hedgerow losses. It was not possible to establish crop patterns with sufficient accuracy from a ground survey with access only on rights of way.

The information from air photos was supplemented by three important additional sources: The parish summaries of the Agricultural Census were helpful, although, since the study area includes parts of three parishes, the Agricultural Census can be used only as confirmatory and supplementary evidence. Ordnance Survey maps of 2500:1 and 10,000:1 of several dates were used. These were particularly useful for identifying ponds. An additional source of data was local knowledge and local informants; for example, about dates of pond drainage and changes in farm ownership or management. In fact most ponds were not drained but simply abandoned and allowed to silt up after the arrival of mains water in the late 1940s. With the aid of Ministry grants for farm supply, increased capitalization of livestock husbandry methods and a reduction of livestock at the expense of cereals overall, the functional need for ponds rapidly disappeared.

The information on the whole area is presented in Table 3.1. Figures 3.2a and 3.2b present the information in a more visual form for a northerly section of approximately one-tenth of the whole area. The information for this part of the area is also summarized in Table 3.1. It would not be possible to present the information in mapped form in sufficient detail over the whole 20

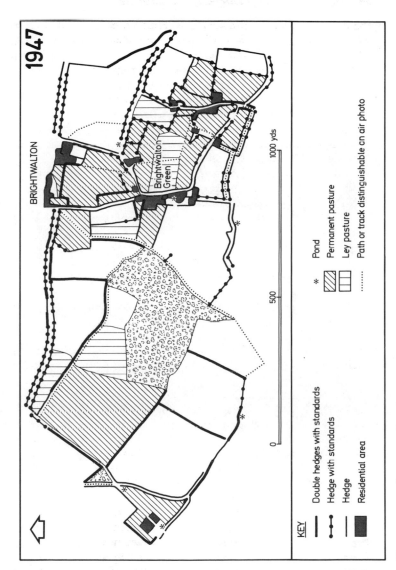

1947

BRIGHTWALTON

Brightwalton
Green

KEY

Double hedges with standards

Hedge with standards

Hedge

Residential area

*   Pond

Permanent pasture

Ley pasture

.... Path or track distinguishable on air photo

0   500   1000 yds

Figure 3.2a   Subsection of study area: 1947

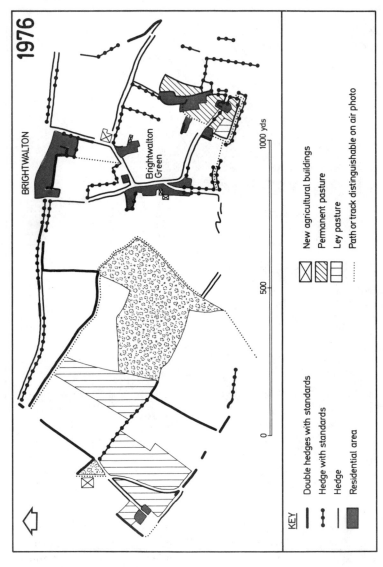

Figure 3.2b Subsection of study area: 1976

square kilometres but a map does help to make the real extent of change easier to grasp.

Even a map, however, does not convey some features of change. An important case is hedgerow degradation. It is not just that hedgerows have been grubbed out. In this part of West Berkshire hedgerow grubbing was mainly over by the mid-1970s (though there are still examples occurring). Hedgerows have also become very much degraded by neglect and, more particularly, careless maintenance with flail cutters. Thus even where hedges are shown in 1976 or 1981, many of them are sparse and tatty without much visual appeal or value as wildlife habitat. The process was exacerbated in the 1970s by Dutch elm disease which killed hundreds of hedgerow standards and also ruined some of the most important stretches of thick double hedge, such as that running due south to Spray Wood from the Woolley/Brightwalton road. This hedge, which was a thick double hedge of elm saplings providing shelter to game and wildlife, now provides a sickly sight in a sick countryside. But the hedge on the southern side of the Woolley/Brightwalton road has simply given up the ghost and disappeared in the face of ill treatment. There, only the three standards, in this case beech, are left to provide a new class of hedge, standards only. There are other examples in the area of this new landscape form: a visual break with little or no potential for wildlife or game.

The overall changes are typical of those in lowland England. There has been a huge increase in mechanization and intensity of cultivation associated with increased specialization, increases in farm size and reduction in labour and employment. The parish summaries of the Agricultural Census for the three parishes in which the survey area lies, show that agricultural full-time employment fell from 99 in 1947 to 64 in 1963 and 28 in 1980. These changes have gone together with a huge increase in tillage, especially cereals, loss of permanent pasture and of visible paths and tracks. The move to specialization, although apparent overall, is partially offset by two of the largest farms in the area, the result of amalgamation and absorption, which now operate intensive mixed farm systems with livestock housed for much or all of the year in covered yards or cowsheds, coupled with ley pastures and cereals. Another offsetting factor has been an increase in 'horseyculture' after the rapid decline of the working horse after the Second World War. This is not just confined to small paddocks around the villages. There is also a stud farm at Chaddleworth.

The land uses identified in Table 3.1 do not exhaust the entire 20 square kilometres since the area devoted to a number of uses is not given. Hedges and tracks are measured linearly; their area is not given. The small part of the defence establishment, already mentioned, is excluded as is the area of roads. Also excluded are small industrial areas outside the villages and farm buildings. Thus the builders' yard at Brightwalton Green is included in the residential area but the area of Thames Water Board boreholes sunk in the 1970s is excluded as is the area of disused pits and quarries except where those are wooded over, when they are measured as woodland. Many of the old chalk pits in the area are on field boundaries and are incorporated in the length of hedges. There probably remains also some measurement error, though cross checks with Ordnance Survey area estimates where available suggest these are not significant.

In aggregate the agricultural area changed little from 1947 to 1981, despite an increase in the residential area by nearly half and a more than eleven-fold increase in the recreational area. In 1947 the agricultural area extended to 1652.5 hectares (82.6 per cent of the total); in 1976 there was a slight reduction to 1626 hectares (81.2 per cent). The reduction in agricultural acreage of 25.9 hectares was less than the combined increase of 55.7 hectares in the residential and recreational areas because of the loss of woodland (12.3 hectares), hedges and tracks.

Within the agricultural area, the pattern of change was more or less typical of southern England: arable increased by nearly 40 per cent; permanent pasture decreased to little more than one-fifth of the immediate post-war area; and there was a significant increase in short-term ley pastures. The division between short-term leys and permanent pasture is always to an extent arbitrary and, perhaps, in interpretation from air photos, more so than on the ground. The distinction was made on visual evidence, ley pasture having a much more homogeneous appearance and being without darker patches of weeds or scrub.

In 1947 there were three significant expanses of chalk down-land type pasture left; two on the western strip and one on the east, on the slope above the Wantage/Newbury road. All three had gone by 1976. Otherwise at both dates the permanent pasture was concentrated in small enclosures around and amongst the settlements. This was probably a pattern derived from the need for easy access to livestock, particularly working horses, milking cows and young livestock that needed a constant eye.

The result of this inheritance, coupled with planners' concerns, is that a very high proportion of the extension of the residential area has been on to these small enclosures both in the course of 'infilling' and, as the detailed maps of development at Brightwalton Green, Figures 3.3a and 3.3b, reveal, via annexation. Since the total extension of the residential area was less than 28 hectares, compared with a loss of nearly 450 hectares of permanent pasture, it is clear, however, that agricultural change is overwhelmingly the most important agent. The islands of permanent pasture in which the settlements lay were simply engulfed by the advancing cereal tide.

The arable area, at both dates, consisted almost exclusively of cereals. The date of the 1947 air mosaic allows this to be identified with some certainty since cereal fields in process of harvest and just after harvest show up well. In 1976 the photographic evidence coupled with local knowledge was adequate for identification. In 1947 there were a few isolated fields of other arable crops, possibly brassicas. In 1976, thanks to the financial inducements of CAP, there was a significant area of rape.

These changes in agriculture are typical of the moves to intensification analysed elsewhere. In terms of the social costs there is a vicious circle. Subsidies induce prosperity, which in turn increases agricultural rents and land prices and produces intensification; this leads, given the subsidies on capital inputs, to the use of yet more capital, greater prosperity and more intensification. At the same time unsubsidized labour is being substituted out of the system and, with specialization, more chemical inputs are being substituted for natural inputs and control by rotation. This then leads to yet further intensification, environmental costs and landscape change.

Hedges are a good example. To maintain them properly as stock proof barriers requires a significant amount of labour which was being rapidly substituted out of agriculture. At the same time arable monoculture has no use for stock proof barriers and without proper maintenance, rotations and grazing, hedges, which are the reservoir of natural flora, can produce a weed

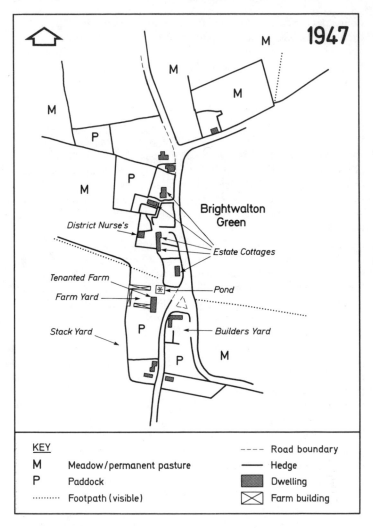

KEY

M   Meadow/permanent pasture

P   Paddock

....   Footpath (visible)

- - - -   Road boundary

——   Hedge

▨   Dwelling

⊠   Farm building

Figure 3.3a   Brightwalton Green: detail, 1947

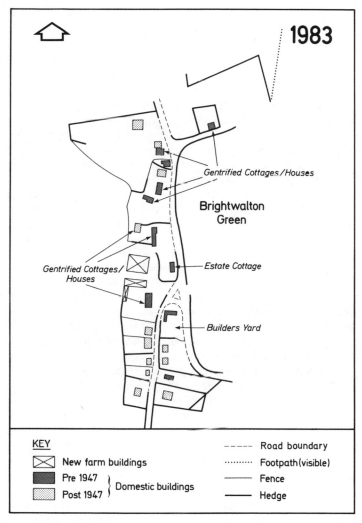

KEY

⊠ New farm buildings

▓ Pre 1947 ⎫
▒ Post 1947 ⎭ Domestic buildings

----- Road boundary
.... Footpath (visible)
——— Fence
▬▬▬ Hedge

Figure 3.3b Brightwalton Green: detail, 1983

control problem. Couple this with the subsidies given to capital, leading to ever larger machines needing bigger fields and economizing on unsubsidized labour and the subsidy-induced rise in land prices/rents which increases the opportunity cost of leaving 'unproductive' hedges and other odd corners undisturbed, and there is a formidable financial incentive to grub out hedges. Add to this an 'improvement' grant which in real terms often pays more than the actual costs of taking the hedges out (this can be done in off seasons using machines and labour which would be paid for anyway) and surprise at hedgerow grubbing completely disappears.

In the study area of West Berkshire a substantial length of hedge has been lost, nearly 55 out of an original 129 km in 1947. The proportionate loss of thicker hedgerows with standard trees in them has been slightly greater overall. The degradation of remaining hedgerows, though more difficult to quantify, is particularly striking and needs re-emphasizing. Since the early 1970s, with cumulative neglect and then Dutch elm disease, this erosion of the aesthetic quality and wildlife value of hedges has proceeded at a frightening pace.

It is often argued that hedge loss is now a thing of the past because all those that 'need' to go have now gone. We can see from the evidence of West Berkshire that this is not necessarily true. Not only is there the continuing erosion of hedgerow quality, which ultimately leads to the death of the hedge, but hedge grubbing occurs at different times in different areas.

Partly this is connected with the timing of changes in management discussed below, partly no doubt with soil type which, in combination with climate, has largely determined the inherited field patterns and the traditional local agricultural systems that have been broken down since 1947. As a result of these factors, enlargement of fields, arable and intensification have tended to spread from the east across lowland England. So it may have been true, even in the mid-1960s, that in eastern counties, such as Huntingdonshire and Cambridgeshire, hedges had already largely been removed. Yet as the 1963 air photos reveal, in West Berkshire agricultural change had hardly started. Indeed it was primarily for that reason that they were not analysed separately since, apart from some loss of permanent pasture and extension of cereal cultivation, there was by that date comparatively little to document. So although in West Berkshire hedgerow grubbing (as opposed to degradation) may indeed be nearly at an end, one is left with the suspicion that further west there may still be much hedgerow to be lost if present policies are continued. New livestock systems, such as zero grazing, with livestock being kept inside all the time, depending on capitalization and producing intensification to the same extent as specialized cereal growing, can likewise have no use for hedges and the machinery used may find bigger fields an advantage.

Apart from the increase in machinery size, another aspect of agricultural intensification in West Berkshire is capital investment in new buildings. Examples of these new buildings are shown in Figure 3.3b, which illustrates details of changes in a small area around Brightwalton Green. There are many others in the overall area, however; seven in the subsection illustrated in Figure 3.2. Just as other eras of agricultural prosperity are linked with new building – the era of Parliamentary enclosures, of early nineteenth-century improvement or 1860/70 Victorian high farming – so the post-war period of subsidy-induced prosperity has produced its rash of new building. Unlike the traditional structures of the past, which in West Berkshire would have been built of local brick and thatched or tiled, slowly mellowing into the landscape, the new agricultural buildings are all but universally made of corrugated asbestos. The very best that can be said of the aesthetic qualities of this material is that with time, it can acquire a certain drabness that means it no longer stands out like a sore thumb.

These new buildings, just like the other changes already detailed, are the product of subsidy-induced prosperity and change. Apart from the grants and tax relief available (and the anomalous exemption from planning procedures well documented by Shoard[3]) they are the adjuncts of the new agricultural systems brought into being. One of the major building types is covered yards and other housing for cattle raised under cover and fed silage, prepared and bought-in feed, or cut grass. This, coupled with ploughing and seeding pastures, intensive cereal production to provide the bought-in feed and increased use of chemical fertilizers (themselves subsidized up to half their cost for most of the period), insecticides and herbicides, allows and increases the intensification of land use and elimination of hedges.

It is not, of course, just the agricultural landscape which has changed in isolation. Ownership and control, too, have been changing. The main agricultural changes in this area of West Berkshire started in the 1960s. The usual pattern in this area seems to have been that a change of management occurred – a new tenant or a farm sale – following which there was a rapid spate of 'improvement'. Examples of this in the area covered by the detailed map are the amalgamation of Green farm with Manor farm in the mid-1960s, or the sale of Malthouse farm by its traditional family owners in the late 1950s. Thus from one point of view, rural change can appear to be a problem of 'management', which may be modified by appeals to the better nature of those who control land, education or whatever. In fact this is far too superficial a diagnosis. The change, although it happens in sudden spurts in any one place, happens continuously in the aggregate and it follows the manipulation of economic conditions, the subsidized route of policy.

That it coincides so often with managerial change is not surprising. The agricultural systems and crops favoured by policymakers are, to traditional farmers, 'new'. In addition, the traditional farmers, as the work of Newby[4] has shown, tend to be more sympathetic to what may be called 'conservation': they place a greater importance on the appearance of the countryside and on wildlife. They are in a position to derive a direct benefit from the appearance of the countryside. Thus not only are they less likely to be able to apply the methods to which the policy structure is geared and from which maximum profit may be derived, they might be less willing to do so even if they could. As long as they are owner occupiers or paying fixed rents, below the market level, they can absorb their non-profit maximizing behaviour and, depending on their tastes, derive a non-pecuniary rent from their farming techniques which produce a more attractive landscape and more varied fauna and flora. What they cannot do is compete in the relatively competitive land market for farm sales or new tenancies because, given the subsidy system, their techniques could not produce the necessary money income to service their capital.

Agribusinessmen, or even more obviously farm managers, installed by outside financial interests that acquire land for investment purposes, are not only likely to be better schooled in how to maximize financial returns within the rules of the game established by the subsidy system; they are also likely to derive less non-pecuniary benefit from the appearance of the country-side. This is most obvious in the case of non-agricultural money – investment funds – drawn into agricultural land because of the subsidy-induced post-war prosperity which, as is shown elsewhere, has led to spiralling land values well ahead of inflation. Here the absentee, impersonal owner derives no benefit whatsoever from the appearance of the landscape and so the management aim is likely to be to maximize financial returns at the expense of all other considerations.

There is thus yet another twist to the vicious circle. The amount of public money pumped into agriculture since the war has increased the returns from farming. This, in turn, has pushed up land values. Together these factors, as in previous eras of prosperity, have attracted outside investment. But unlike the era of 'improvement' of the first decade or so of the nineteenth century when agricultural prosperity drew in the money of the emerging industrial capitalists seeking the prestige of land ownership as well as a good investment, this new inflow of money is largely unconcerned with the attributes of land ownership other than the purely financial. An investment fund manager is not going to have his farm managers plant up game coverts, establish parklands or go in for major schemes of amenity tree planting at the expense of financial returns. The only exception to this may be the interest of some agribusinessmen in shooting. Thus policy is not only causing directly the detrimental changes in the country-side documented in this chapter. Indirectly it is, in addition, causing a substitution of ownership.

A group of traditional owners, at least some of whom valued personally the non-marketable attributes of the countryside valued by society at large and who farmed in traditional ways, is being squeezed out by the very prosperity they have called for. A new group is moving in, members of which, as Newby has shown,[5] place little value on 'conservation' and who anyway are compelled by the financial logic they are themselves exploiting, to ignore any consideration but the purely financial. But it is not the changing ownership which is the cause. Underlying it all is the system of support and subsidy brought into being by the supposed guardians of the public interest.

Alongside this change in the agricultural community is another change in the area. The old rural community has been progressively displaced by new commuters, rich retired and weekenders. This process is part of the pattern of urban decentralization that has been going on throughout the developed world since the Second World War. In Britain the decentralization of manufacturing industry has been in progress since the 1950s and the decentralization of population, as distinct from its suburbanization, has been a general pattern since the 1960s. Its extent, already apparent to students of the phenomenon, has been revealed in the 1981 Census.[6] This shows that in the 1970s the areas with the fastest rates of growth of population were the most rural parts of Britain within reach of major cities. West Sussex and West Berkshire were two of the fastest growing, for example, and that growth is well illustrated in the study area. Agricultural change, as already stated, really got underway in the 1960s; social and economic change accelerated very rapidly with the opening of the M4 late in 1972. Overnight this moved the area within an hour of London by road, compared to its previous three hours.

Figure 3.3b illustrates the physical process in a small part of the study area, though what happened there is more or less typical of what happened elsewhere. The pattern of decentralization has been for the relatively less affluent to concentrate in the larger centres, such as Newbury, and the villages to become the preserve of the rich. After the war there was some rural council house building in the area, most notably at Chaddleworth. The largest employer of manual workers in the area is the defence establishment already noted just south of Chaddleworth. No council houses have been built since the 1950s and most of the old estate cottages have been sold off as opportunity arose. Thus working-class housing has been declining. So, too, of course, has working-class employment. Apart from the decline in agricultural employment already referred to, other employers of manual workers, such as traditional craft industries, have gone out of business. For example, employment associated with coppicing still survived in the area until the early 1950s. There was also a coach depot in one of the villages until the early 1970s. Other manual employment has been stifled by planning policies. A successful local transport firm, based in one of the villages and developed from the original village carters, was forced to relocate on the Thatcham industrial estate when it wanted to expand in the 1970s. Its premises have now been built over for desirable executive housing – part of the deal with the planners.

The result of these changes, as in most of England and Wales, has been a slow retreat of the indigenous rural inhabitants into a few rural council houses (which themselves are being sold off), the surviving estate cottages and the local towns, such as Newbury. The main exceptions are the village builders and their families who find ample employment in 'gentrifying' the cottages for their new owners.

The incomers have arrived in several more or less distinct waves. The first to arrive in the 1960s were the better off local businessmen. The area acted as a prosperous suburb for Newbury and Wantage. Older houses were extended and frequently small paddocks were built in or annexed into gardens from agricultural use. Two examples of this can be seen in Figure 3.3b. This process was often concurrent with farm amalgamations or changes of ownership. Another group of the 1960s, often in relatively small houses in 'in-fill' plots, was not so affluent retired people.

Spurred by the opening of the M4, there was a large inflow of middle-and upper-middle income executives and professionals in the early 1970s. At more or less the same time came an inflow of extremely well-off weekenders (house prices in the area ensured that only the really rich could afford its weekend cottages) and rich retired people. Figure 3.3b shows several examples. Again the pattern was for traditional rows of one-up one-down workers' cottages to be knocked together to form a single dwelling; for extensions and some further in-fill development, distinctly up market from that of the 1960s.

The interaction of these social and economic changes with the agricultural changes this chapter mainly documents is interesting. Underlying it was the decline of the traditional rural economy, much hastened by capitalization and mechanization, which reduced working-class employment in the countryside, and also, as a result, tended to release housing. The mechanization and other changes in agricultural systems meant that farmers had increasingly little use for small enclosures and paddocks, such as those shown in Figure 3.3a, which were taken into gardens. In addition, a farmhouse sold off with a paddock or more land commanded a more than proportionate premium with the new class of purchasers. In some cases the paddocks might provide grazing for a horse, the key status symbol of the ex-urbanizing countryside; in others they might simply be incorporated into gardens to provide grounds commensurate with the new extended size of the houses and space perhaps for a swimming pool; or in yet other cases they might be sold off later for in-fill development at a handsome profit.

Apart from the transfer of paddocks, there is another form of annexation even more closely bound up with agricultural changes. Figure 3.3b illustrates two examples where field boundaries have been rounded off and margins taken into gardens. With the ever-increasing size of machines, odd corners which involved time- and fuel-consuming manoeuvring to cultivate became of increasingly limited agricultural value. In some instances small corners were even neglected altogether but in the area around the settlements, with their new affluent occupiers, opportunities were not missed to buy up the now all but useless agricultural space. Where the 24-foot combine cannot reach, the ride-on tractor mower can happily go. Supply was determined by agricultural change; demand by social and economic change.

Another change in the local area which relates, in part, to the social and economic ones, is the disuse of tracks and footpaths. In terms of visible length, as opposed to the length of legal rights of way, we can see that over the period as a whole there was a loss of over half the total. Very largely this resulted from agricultural change. Footpaths often followed hedges and the loss of hedge led to the loss of both path and hedge. The whole area formerly occupied by path and hedge would usually be brought under the plough. Another factor is the growth generally of the tillage area and particularly the loss of permanent pasture. Paths across permanent pasture stay and their visible existence encourages their use. A public footpath sign pointing across a freshly ploughed field or an expanse of ripening cereals, is not nearly so encouraging. In addition, public footpaths signs, like the physical existence of the footpaths themselves, have a habit of disappearing. Between 1975 and 1977 all paths in the area were waymarked by the local Ramblers' Association with signs provided by the County Council. By 1981 a good proportion of the signs had been removed or, for other reasons, had disappeared.

This loss of physical public rights of way over the countryside is associated with the social and economic changes because the new inhabitants simply do not know where the paths were nor do they have the confidence to head off across a newly sown field knowing that that is what has always been done. Increased use of cars and the erosion of the need to use footpaths has often been cited as a reason for their loss. It has probably played a part but not as great a part, perhaps, as is often, especially by the farming community, ascribed to it. For some paths a practical need remains; the elderly, and mothers with young children in one-car households, frequently still walk as a practical means of transport. A right of way running from Brightwalton Green to the only post office in the area at Chaddleworth would not only be the shortest and most pleasant route for many, it would also, given the high banked narrow lanes, be by far the safest. However, the path, though visibly used alongside the hedge in 1947, had long since disappeared in 1981. Not only that, but while the practical use of paths has undoubtedly declined, their leisure use has boomed. The well-signed and known Ridgeway, which passes 6 km to the north of the area, can be as crowded with walkers as a city pavement on a sunny Sunday afternoon.

This area of West Berkshire has thus seen most of the changes which typify post-war agricultural 'improvement' and rural gentrification. The loss of ponds was briefly alluded to earlier. It has been considerable. Of the 25 ponds in the area in 1947, 17 had disappeared by 1981 and of those remaining many, like the hedges, were degraded. They had become silted up and overgrown. Although the subsidy system has played a part, with its encouragement of intensive livestock systems for which ponds are unsuitable and the grants offered to farmers, often attached to other 'improvement', for mains water, probably a high proportion of the pond loss would have happened anyway. Independently of agricultural subsidies, mains water was, inexorably, reaching the most outlying parts of England and Wales by the mid-twentieth century. The loss of ponds has nevertheless had a severe impact on wildlife. Not only, in conjunction with pesticides, has it been associated with the virtual elimination of the now uncommon frog from lowland England (it is now easier to find frogs in suburban gardens than in much of the English countryside), but with much other wildlife too. Swallows, for example, disappeared from the immediate area of Brightwalton Green illustrated in Figures 3.3a and b within three years of the pond being filled in prior to the building of the new straw store.

The most recent change that has become important is woodland loss. The first example within this area of West Berkshire was Chaddleworth Common copse which was cleared in the late 1960s. By the mid-1970s the land was being used as a commercial golf course. This, together with two small recreation fields, accounts for the eleven-fold increase in the recreational area since 1947. This caters for the new, relatively leisured and rich inhabitants of West Berkshire.

The next to go was two-thirds of the extent of Field Copse, the largest stand of woodland in the area – and not only the largest but from all the evidence one of, if not the, oldest. The woodland was mentioned in the records of Abingdon Abbey in the twelfth century and from the field and farm names around it, such as Purley Farm and Purley Common, was apparently part of the medieval woodland. Given this evidence, it is probable that it had been continuously woodland since before the original human settlement of the area, having been brought into the medieval system and worked continuously with various clearings and plantings as coppice till after the Second World War. It was then retained by its owners as an amenity and *de facto* nature reserve since it was not used for shooting and casual access was allowed for all local people. There was a large herd of fallow deer and two badger sets, as well as several now uncommon but not rare bird species, such as barn owls and sparrow hawks, besides all the more usual woodland species. Not being shot, it contained an abundance of birds, such as magpies and jays, surprisingly uncommon now in intensively farmed and shot southern England.

In 1976 Field Copse was bought and most grubbed out to extend yet further the cereal acreage. The connection with agricultural policy hardly needs spelling out. Apart from the inflated value of agricultural land compared to woodland and the induced intensification of agriculture, there was a direct EEC grant available to pay 60 per cent of the costs of clearance. It is probable that more woodland will go in the future unless present policies are changed, since that which remains does not yield the same returns as subsidized agriculture and much depends on the personal taste (and independent wealth) of current landowners, many of whom use their woodland for game.

What we can see in this area of West Berkshire exemplifies most of the changes in the British countryside induced by agricultural change since the war. We can see, too, how agricultural change has interacted with, and to an extent been reinforced by, rural gentrification. The farming lobby, particularly in voicing their opposition to public access to the countryside, are apt to make the rhetorical point that the fields are their factory floor and how would an industrialist like it if the public were allowed to wander in at will. There is increasingly a sense of sardonic truth to this comparison. Not only are we as a community paying farmers to produce fields which have little more charm and less wildlife than factories, but the city is itself, as has been remarked elsewhere, coming to the countryside.[7] In traditional senses of the word it is becoming inappropriate to call areas such as this part of West Berkshire rural. Policy has had a part, though not the major one, in turning the settlements into high-income residential subdivisions. Policy has played the key role in bringing about the agricultural changes, the effect of which has been greatly to reduce the social benefits, amenity value and environmental quality of the countryside; which is what the incoming city, which provides the support, was coming to find.

Notes

1 Shoard, M. (1980) *The Theft of the Countryside*, London, Temple Smith.
2 Hardy, T. (1895) *Jude the Obscure*, 1st edn, London, Osgood, McIlraine.
3 Shoard (1980), op. cit.
4 Newby, H., Bell, C. and Rose, D. (1977) 'Farmers' Attitudes to Conservation', *Countryside Recreation Review*, vol. 2.
5 Newby, Bell and Rose (1977), op. cit.
6 See, for example, *1981 Census of Population: Preliminary Report, England and Wales* (1982), Table B, London, HMSO.
7 Leven, C. L. (ed.) (1978) *The Mature Metropolis*, Farnborough, Hants., D. C. Heath.

4

From rags to riches or what the government has done for farmers and what farmers have done for us

In the last 200 years two social groups stand out for their phenomenal advancement up the ladder of social prestige and economic reward. Doctors have advanced from being 'leeches' or 'sawbones' – barbers with ideas above their station in life – to the high priests we know today. Farmers have transformed themselves from their virtual peasant status of the eighteenth century to the exalted and romanticized position they occupy today. An urbane and liberal-minded economist of the early nineteenth century, David Ricardo, could write contemptuously:

> It has been justly observed that no reduction would take place in the price of corn although landlords should forego the whole of their rent. Such a measure would only enable some farmers to live like gentlemen.[1]

This change in their status has gone hand in hand with changes in land tenure, farmers' economic position and their political influence. Perhaps non-coincidentally it has also gone with a mass exodus from the land as a means of earning a living, with urbanization and, now, suburbanization. The romanticized picture of farming presented in TV advertisements and children's books in the 1980s would have been quite impossible to project 200 years ago – not only for the obvious technological reasons but because the mass of the population was too close to the reality. This transformation has been achieved surprisingly recently. The social perception of farmers in the 1920s and 1930s, as can be seen from a book like *Akenfield*,[2] was still not dissimilar to that in the USA and parts of Europe today – hayseeds, country hicks or peasants. This still reflected the traditional role of farmers: men to whom landlords let land or to whom they 'farmed' out the dirty business of producing food from the soil. In 1922 it was still the case that nearly five times as much land was rented as owned outright and farmers suffered from the depression of that decade as much or more than any other group. By 1960 owner occupiers outnumbered tenants and the word 'farmer' had almost inverted its original meaning. To most people the word probably now indicates an owner of land.

As the final section of this chapter shows, this change in land tenure and growth of owner occupation has been accompanied by as complete a transformation of the place of farmers in the income hierarchy. It is the means by which this latter change was effected that we wish to examine in this chapter. It is perhaps a mild irony worth noting, however, that a new factor which may ultimately reverse this development, but which in part at least owes its origin to the very success of farmers, is already visible. This is the growing institutional ownership of land, discussed in Chapter 8, and the consequent creation of a new class of landless farmers, the 'farm managers'.

Both the transformation of the ownership structure of land, which has been associated with an upward movement of farmers in the wealth distribution, and the transformation of the price and cost structure of agriculture which has boosted their position in the income distribution, have stemmed from government intervention. This may be regarded as ironic, since farmers who as a body are more against government and its doings than most others, have benefited from those doings proportionately more. The transformation of land ownership owes something to the tax structure and its effects on inheritance and changes in the legal position of tenants *vis-à-vis* landlords. The change in farmers' incomes has been brought about directly by government intervention in agricultural markets and support for agriculture. In the pursuit of this last activity government has not only transformed the incomes of farmers (and thus, as Ricardo would have recognized, further increased the value of existing landowners' holdings – and so farmers' wealth) but has also, almost unawares, contributed largely to the disastrous changes in the countryside already documented. It is therefore to this development that we now turn.

The management of agricultural markets in Britain really dates from the Second World War; though, perhaps, some aspects are rooted further in the past – the experience of the post-1918 recovery and the inter-war period. For some 20 years after the Second World War the outlook, objectives and the machinery for implementing agricultural policy remained essentially unchanged. In the early 1970s, however, two changes came in quick succession: first the adoption of the EEC Common Agricultural Policy (CAP) with its rather different aims and quite different machinery; and second the temporary sharp rise of world commodity prices which briefly reversed a trend of 20 years when commodity prices had been falling relative to those of manufactured goods. For a short time this swept agricultural markets out of government control. Although falling prices of commodities in real terms and pressure from the western European farmers' lobby have succeeded in re-establishing a substantial degree of protection, the breaking of a long-term trend temporarily created an air of uncertainty.

The historical background to protection

In Britain output was comparatively unaffected by the First World War, but in Europe as a whole agriculture suffered devastating effects. There was a fall in total production of about one-third. This decline in output was further aggravated from the British point of view by the disappearance of Russian supplies from world markets. Before 1917 Russia was one of the major sources of British wheat imports, but the revolution meant that these supplies were no longer available. This reduction in European supplies was partly compensated for by a vast increase in output in other countries, which had responded to the war shortage and the high prices in Europe. The USA, for example, which by 1913 had almost thrown off its nineteenth-century role of agricultural exporter, six years later had increased its wheat acreage by half and had become again a major source of supply for Europe. Canada had doubled its pre-war acreage by 1919.

But this increase in production outside Europe was only a partial substitute for the loss within Europe. There was a world shortage of food and, since the half-hearted attempts at rationing had little effect, it was directly reflected in British prices. In 1914 the price index for all agricultural produce in England and Wales stood at 111 (1906–8 = 100); it reached its post-war peak in 1920 when it was 321. Prices thus rose by almost 200 per cent in just seven years.

This sharp rise in the level of agricultural prices could not, however, last. It only reflected the temporary world shortage of food caused by the European war and as men returned to the land and horses were released from requisition, farmers tempted by high prices, cajoled by governments, and aided by technical developments, increased their output. By the late 1920s European production had recovered to pre-war levels whilst production in the main exporting countries greatly exceeded that of the pre-war period. The result, of course, from the farmers' point of view was catastrophic. Prices collapsed from their 1920 level to hardly more than half that level by 1923 and the price index reached a low of 123 in 1933 when the world surplus of food resulting from the return to 'normality' of European production and the continuing 'wartime' level of production in the exporting countries was compounded by the international depression.

The acute depression in agriculture in the 1930s was, therefore, not just a symptom of the international slump but had its origin in the changes brought about by the First World War and the post-war boom. Certainly, as Figure 4.1 shows, the decline in agricultural prices started a long time before the depression proper.

The impact of the depression on agriculture and on the British countryside was predictable. The intensity of cultivation fell off and investment and maintenance all but ceased. The acreage of permanent grass, for example, which had risen more or less steadily since the boom decade of the 1860s to reach 17,606,000 acres in 1914 had fallen to 15,782,000 in 1919 as a result of the war and post-war boom; thereafter as prices fell so the acreage expanded again to reach 17,410,000 acres in 1938. Similarly the number of sheep rose from 19,744,000 in 1920 to 25,882,000 in 1938. Following its traditional pattern British agriculture retreated to sheep and permanent pasture in response to a slump in the industry.

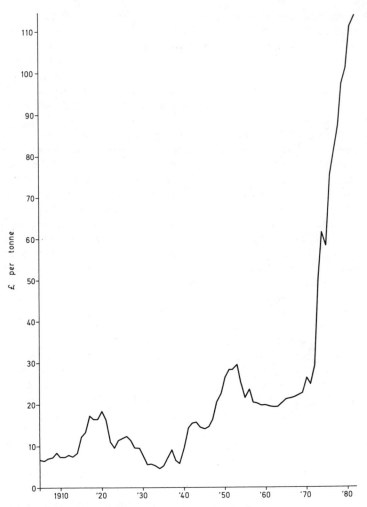

Figure 4.1   Wheat prices: 1905–82;[1] £ per tonne[2]

Source: Corn returns.

1 Prices exclude deficiency payments; those for 1980 to 1982 are provisional.
2 Current prices.

Naturally, factors other than the general prosperity of agriculture have affected sheep numbers; the particular prosperity of sheep, for example, and also weather and disease. The growth of the New Zealand lamb trade and then, more recently, the declining significance of wool, have been influential. But from the 1890s through to 1940 these factors were relatively constant and Figure 4.2 charts the rise and fall in sheep numbers as farming in general and arable in particular became less or more prosperous. The general pattern was accentuated in 1940 when the traditional influence of prosperity was reinforced by directives from the Ministry of Agriculture, and the two combined to achieve a slaughter of sheep the like of which had never been seen before. The sheep population fell by one quarter between 1939 and 1944. Thus with a little imagination one can visualize the power of the abstract forces of the 'invisible hand' literally to transform the physical appearance of the countryside.

But just as prosperity, rapacity and over-capitalization ravage the British countryside today, in the great depression the lack of investment and maintenance appalled. The crumbling walls and buildings, unkempt hedges and weed- (and flower-) infested fields led a contemporary writer to lament:

> Everywhere you find . . . buildings in a deplorable state, roofs defective, doors broken down and the walls often affording but little shelter. The farm roads are neglected and the farmyards in wet weather are deep in slush and liquid manure; the gates are broken down, or patched up anyhow, and the fields often enough, with their vistas of weeds and rubbish, cry aloud for land drainage.[3]

Farmers' economic circumstances were shaping the countryside.

The depression in agriculture in the 1930s was an important influence on those who formulated agricultural policy after the Second World War. Even before the war the case for relieving agriculture from the undamped impact of market forces was being argued and to a limited extent implemented. (Interestingly Addison, the writer of the preceding extract, who was one of those both arguing for, and as minister implementing, government intervention, did so on, amongst other grounds, the importance of a prosperous agriculture in maintaining the beauty and appeal of the landscape:

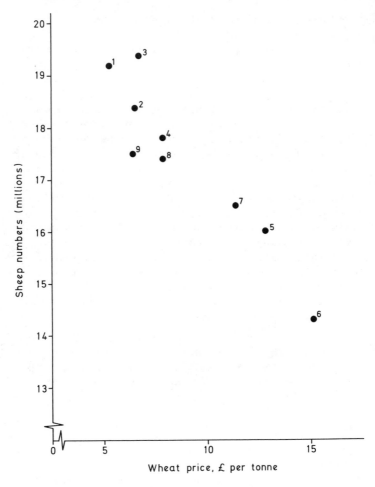

Figure 4.2 Sheep numbers and wheat prices, England and Wales, 1893–1940[1]

Source: Ministry of Agriculture, Fisheries and Food (1968) *A Century of Agricultural Statistics*, London, HMSO.

1 Data relate to means for five-year periods; sheep numbers lagged three years.

There is one fact that never comes into agricultural talks, but which we ought not to forget. The British landscape we love so much has been preserved by farming. The pasturelands, the fields and hedges bespeak generations of loving care . . . the neglect . . . should help us to realize what things would be like if it were not for farming – thistles, nettles and weeds and all manner of rubbish spreading over good land offending the eye.

For the period in which he wrote he was doubtless right. Now perhaps we should write 'used to be preserved by farming' for 'has been'.)

In the late 1920s farming, which already enjoyed partial relief, was granted the 100 per cent rate relief which it still enjoys today. But more direct supports were provided first by means of tariff and quota protection in 1931 and later by the establishment of marketing boards. What agriculture, as a result of its structure – a very large number of small and frequently uncooperative units – was unable to do, the government began to do for it. Mechanisms were provided, in the name of controlling price fluctuations, for regulating output and thus maintaining prices. But many people, including the writer just referred to, wanted the government to go much further in supporting and controlling the industry.

Events secured this aim with great rapidity. The onset of the Second World War immediately promoted agriculture to the status of a high priority strategic industry. Every ton of wheat grown in Great Britain meant one less ton imported and so more valuable shipping space available for other strategic supplies. In a siege situation this U-boat policy for agriculture made sense and the aim was maximum output (particularly of bulk foods such as potatoes and cereals) before all else. The industry was almost overwhelmed with government exhortation and aid.

In just three years from 1938–9 to 1941–2 the value of gross output soared by two-thirds; this was the farmers' contribution to the war effort, a moral account on which they were able to draw heavily for public support when the war ended. But their contribution was to an important extent visible only on paper. If account is taken of the rising prices of food, as is done in Figure 4.3, the increase in output was much more modest – some 15 per cent at most. The real contribution was in restructuring output. Indeed, valued at *constant prices* the peak output of 1939–40 was

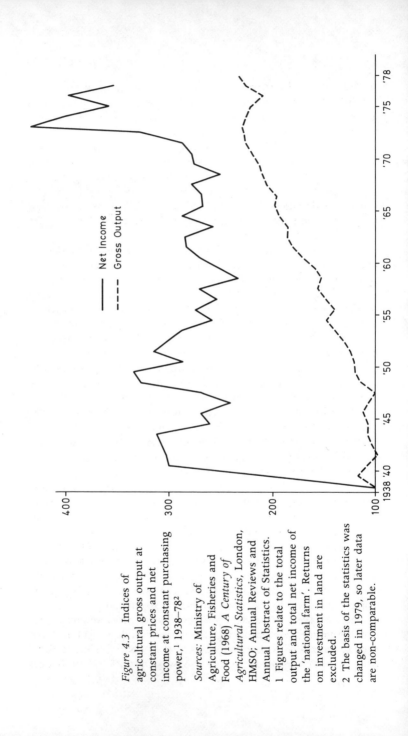

Figure 4.3 Indices of agricultural gross output at constant prices and net income at constant purchasing power,[1] 1938–78[2]

Sources: Ministry of Agriculture, Fisheries and Food (1968) *A Century of Agricultural Statistics*, London, HMSO; Annual Reviews and Annual Abstract of Statistics.

1 Figures relate to the total output and total net income of the 'national farm'. Returns on investment in land are excluded.

2 The basis of the statistics was changed in 1979, so later data are non-comparable.

not reached again until 1949–50. But between 1939 and 1942 physical output of wheat and barley rose by just under two-thirds, that of oats by three-quarters, and output of potatoes almost doubled. Cattle numbers, however, hardly changed – the aim of policy was after all to save imports and this could best be done by saving imported animal feeding stuffs and concentrating on the production of bulk foods whilst rationing more desirable high protein food; and the increased output of the bulk goods was counterbalanced by a reduction of other high value items. The traditional response of British agriculture to prosperity in the form of falling sheep numbers has already been noted.

This prosperity was real enough, as the last section of this chapter demonstrates. The average farmer's real net income more than tripled. It is from this quite recent time that current levels of agricultural prosperity date. It is true that after 1944 the value of farmers' real incomes did not change much until the early 1960s, but when the agricultural lobby was complaining about its pitiful poverty in the late 1960s attention was not drawn to the almost overnight transformation of their status at the start of the Second World War. That war made some less honest fortunes; it also may have made some greater individual fortunes; but as an identifiable group, farmers did better than any other.

The experience of the Second World War provides an interesting comparison with that of the First, both for the similarities and the contrasts. Although the First World War led to prosperity and, consequently, to a certain restructuring of output, it was not so marked as that which took place between 1939 and 1945; partly no doubt, because the depression from which farming recovered was very much worse in 1939 than it had been in 1914. But the rise to prosperity and restructuring of output in the Second World War was achieved with a much smaller change in the level of prices. These had risen by 200 per cent between 1914 and 1921 but from 1939 to 1946 the price index rose not much more than 100 per cent (from 145 to 292). Prices were controlled partly by a relatively efficient and quickly introduced rationing scheme but also by the more successful adjustment of domestic supply.

The effects of the Second World War on supplies in Europe and North America were similar to those of the First. By 1945 European production overall was considerably below that of 1939, while in North America, as during the First World War, there had been a large increase. Outside these two areas, however, the situation was different. The war had been geographically more extensive and large areas of Asia had been affected, whilst in Australia and New Zealand, unlike before, there were no increases in output. This meant that the post-war food shortage was more intense and lasted longer; and this difference had important consequences in shaping post-war agricultural policy.

But equally, or perhaps even more importantly, there was the change in the climate of opinion. After the First World War the government had promised that agricultural support would be permanently established. The promise was ditched, however, as soon as prices dropped with the quick recovery of European production and the general excess in world food supplies which this brought about. Though now more urgently needed by the farmers, support had become too expensive for the government.

After 1945, however, the situation was different. The miserable depression in agriculture and the accompanying rural poverty was still a piece of recent experience and the post-First World War 'betrayal' of agriculture was also remembered. In agriculture, as in other aspects of the post-war recovery, things this time were going to be different. Also, of course, it could already be seen that the post-war food shortage was going to last longer and prices were not going to fall so soon, if at all.

There were furthermore obvious differences in social and political attitudes to such things as government interventions and economic inequality. Despite their recent rise to prosperity, there remained, of course, many small poor farmers and even the large number of larger farmers who had prospered, because their prosperity was so recent, still had not had their changed status registered by society. Thus as a community farmers still had some claim on the egalitarian impulses of the 1945 Labour government. Strategic considerations were also still important in post-war Britain. Most obviously it was argued that the country could not let itself return to its pre-war dependence on imported food for fear of a future war. Yet another argument for agricultural protection was the acute shortage of foreign currency which support for domestic agriculture might possibly relieve. This last argument was one of 'economic strategy', which is discussed in Chapter 7.

One reason why incomes in agriculture have tended since the Industrial Revolution to lag behind those in other sectors is changes in comparative advantage. The Industrial Revolution gave British manufacturers a world lead in their sector. During the late eighteenth and nineteenth centuries this sector grew relative to others. Though British manufacturing's world advantage declined during the later ninetcenth century, it maintained its advantage *vis-à-vis* agriculture. Between 1900 and 1965 employment in agriculture fell by 60 per cent whilst that in manufacturing rose by 50 per cent. More recently it has become the service industry sector that has established a comparative advantage. This massive restructuring of employment, particularly given the inertia of traditional agricultural communities, could only be accomplished in a market system with substantial earnings differentials between sectors.

This is the 'structural' problem of agriculture – a problem not dissimilar to that now faced by a number of manufacturing industries including, for example, the shipbuilding, textile and now steel industries. Historically it has meant that over the whole period of industrialization, agriculture has provided the main reservoir of labour for the growing industries. The lower incomes in agriculture compared to those in other sectors encourage workers to leave the land for other occupations; and from time to time these financial inducements may be bolstered by institutional factors such as at one extreme the wholesale rural dispossession of the enclosures and at the other, such mild measures as the 1967 Agriculture Act, which introduced 'farm structure' grants as an inducement to small farmers to amalgamate their farms or leave farming altogether.

Even in the case of these institutional factors, however, we can see the power of economic forces in transforming the rural economy. The enclosure movement was simply the institutional response to economic pressure, legitimizing the larger land owners' pursuit of profit; the number of Enclosure Acts passed in any one year was mainly determined by the price of corn and cost of capital. Enclosure Acts cost their initiators money, and, as one would expect, their number was a function of their profitability.

Equally, economic forces encouraging people to leave the land may be mitigated. The entire policy of agricultural support is such

an institutional influence which lessens or even, as now, elim-
inates the extent of income differentials between the agricultural
and the industrial and service sectors.

But whether institutional factors are exacerbating or reducing
the impact of income differentials as a means of securing a
redistribution of resources between agriculture, where demand is
stagnating, and other sectors, where until recently at least,
demand was greater, there always remains immobility which
ensures that the actual transfer of resources is one step behind the
transfer of relative demand. Despite the income differentials there
have always tended to be more people in agriculture than are
actually wanted because people are immobile. Indeed one could
argue that if people were perfectly mobile the income differentials
would almost disappear.

This problem of immobility and depressed incomes has tended
to be particularly severe in agriculture because of the structure of
the industry. Typically a manufacturing industry is composed of a
few large firms. If the demand for that industry's output falls then
the few firms in it can contract their output and so keep up the
price for their products, i.e. the loss is mainly borne by the
workers in the form of unemployment. With several hundred
thousand individual farmers agriculture cannot behave in the
same way. One farmer if he reduces his output can have no effect
on agricultural prices since there are all those thousands of other
farmers, so the only way in a market economy that the number of
farmers can decline, apart from 'natural wastage', is by some of
them being forced out of business. This means that farmers, most
of whom now are simultaneously owners and workers, have an
especially strong incentive to combine together as a political
pressure group since they cannot behave like a cartel.

The 1947 Act

The policy of agricultural support which perpetuated the transformation of farmers' economic circumstances effected by the war
was thus the product of various considerations, of historical,
political, social, strategic, economic and perhaps even sentimental
factors. But perhaps the chronically low and uncertain incomes of
farmers resulting from the structural peculiarities of agriculture
described above were the most important single reason why the

Agricultural Act of 1947 came into existence. It was to an extent a matter of chance that support policies should first make their impact in a period of agricultural prosperity unequalled since the early years of the nineteenth century. Hence the need to look back to the 'farmers' betrayal' after the First World War. The new more egalitarian mood recognized the previous injustice and the probability that farmers' recent gains would in time be lost as world agricultural recovery took place. It is also likely that the extent of agriculture's prosperity had not been widely recognized. Apart from estimation difficulties, given their impending government support, it was hardly in farmers' interests to advertise their prosperity; nor given continued financial aid, has that position changed since 1947.

The 1947 Act was a watershed in the history of British agriculture. Farmers were given powerful state interference in the market, sufficient to provide a virtual guarantee of at least a modest prosperity and insulation from economic forces. The Act undertook to provide proper remuneration and living conditions for farmers and workers in agriculture and an adequate return on capital invested in the industry by providing price guarantees for 'such part of the nation's food and other agricultural produce as in the national interest it is desirable to produce in the United Kingdom'. The 'national interest' was not defined in terms of percentages which left a fertile loam in which disputes have flourished ever since.

There are a variety of ways in which farmers' incomes could have been supported other than that which was adopted. These fall into two basic classes: either by guaranteed prices underwritten from a central fund; or the government could impose tariffs or import levies on agricultural produce brought in from more efficient lower cost producing countries, thus bringing up the price of imported food to the level guaranteed to domestic producers. This latter was the method which had been tentatively applied in the 1930s and was continued for the 'non-review' commodities – most importantly for horticultural produce. The Common Market agricultural policy described below is another variety of this basic method. (Where a country is self-sufficient there is a third class, restriction of production. This method is used in the United States where farmers are paid by the government *not* to plant crops over a certain area. The 'support' argument, then, is over how big this 'set aside' acreage should be. In Britain and Europe a variant of this method is used for some crops where we are self-sufficient, e.g. hops, potatoes and liquid milk.)

The policy chosen by the Labour government in 1947 was an example of the former type of policy. Cheaper imported food was allowed to enter the country freely but machinery was provided for paying farmers the difference between the guaranteed price and the market price actually realized when domestic produce was sold in competition with imported food. Under both systems of support the non-farm citizens are subsidizing the farmers; but under what might be called the 'tariff' method the money is provided by people in their role as consumers – the price they pay for their food is inflated by the level of subsidy. With the 'guaranteed price' method the money is raised from the public in their role as taxpayers. Thus since food forms a larger proportion of people's spending the poorer they are, and taxation represents a larger proportion of people's incomes the richer they are, the 'tariff' method of support has a regressive effect, falling most heavily on the poor, and the 'guaranteed price' method has a progressive effect on the distribution of real income. Since the 1947 Act was introduced by a Labour government, one of whose main declared aims was to promote greater fairness, this may have been a factor in determining the type of support system adopted.

But whilst the 1947 Act relied mainly on providing money to support farmers out of higher taxation rather than higher food prices, as seems to be usual with British legislation, it left in existence a large part of the hotch-potch structure of legislation that had been growing up since the First World War to provide special support for agriculture. It appears, as subsequent experience with agricultural support has shown, that it is politically more difficult to take subsidies away from a particular interest group than it is to give them in the first place. The benefits of taking them away will be spread thin over the whole community; the subsidies are large (in the case of agriculture, one should say, extremely large) for a small section. So the small section will go to great lengths to keep subsidies they have got, whereas there is insufficient payoff for any member of the wider community to act. This might be called the ratchet principle of public support. Thus the 1947 Act left untouched the longstanding tax advantages of being a farmer: partial relief from death duty (a relief farmers still enjoy from the tax, the capital transfer tax, which replaced death duty) and the total relief from rates. Many aspects of the tariff protection and the producers' marketing boards of the 1930s were similarly left intact and the marketing boards continued to operate with a legislative mandate.

The 1947 Act added to this existing support a guaranteed price for a series of so-called 'review commodities' whilst allowing the main food products, except fruit and vegetables, free access to the UK market. They were called review commodities because the three ministers responsible for agriculture in the countries of the UK undertook to review annually the condition of agriculture in conjunction with the representatives of the three farmers' unions (but not the agricultural workers). So began the spring rite of the 'price review' with the National Farmers' Union as the only representative industrial body in the country which the government was bound by law to consult when taking decisions which affected it.

The explicit aims of the 1947 policy were to raise farm incomes and to expand British output. A target was set, though not in the Act itself, for a 60 per cent increase in output by 1956 over the average level of the immediate pre-war years. Although increased 'efficiency' was called for, what was meant exactly by 'efficiency' was not publicly defined, nor in general were there any major provisions for achieving it. It was realized that there was a shortage of capital investment in agriculture but the extra income which farmers would secure as a result of the guaranteed prices was thought to be sufficient means of increasing investment. Some of the wartime measures concerned with investment, such as the 'Marginal Production Scheme' designed to help small farmers expand their output, did, however, continue.

Whilst farmers' incomes were increased by the guaranteed prices after the small post-war fall, the policy of expansion was initially a failure. Farmers appeared to be spending their increased incomes on cars and consumption rather than on tractors or investment and thus higher prices led to very little extra output. Between 1945–6 and 1950–1, as Figure 4.3 demonstrates, the value of output at constant prices rose by only about 8.5 per cent. The target of a 60 per cent increase in output over the pre-war average looked a long way off. With the disastrous wheat harvest in 1947, even bread, which had remained off the ration throughout the war, had to be rationed.

Policy in the 1950s

The policymakers' response to this situation was to tie some of the aid received by farmers directly to capital investment, chemical inputs and 'improved' techniques. Before, price support had indirectly provided financial inducements to farmers to farm more intensively and so inimically *vis-à-vis* environmental considerations, as the foregoing discussion of farmers' historical response to prosperity demonstrates. From 1951 on, farmers were paid directly to farm in a way which despoiled the countryside. In that year the first 'production' grant on phosphate fertilizers was introduced. In 1952 this grant was extended to other fertilizers and the basic rate was increased. In addition, two new production grants were introduced. A 'ploughing' grant was offered to farmers as a flat payment for every acre of permanent pasture ploughed up and re-seeded with cultivated strains as temporary grass. The other new grant was on beef calves – this was in addition to the income farmers could realize by selling the animals at the subsidized guaranteed price.

In the terms of the policymakers this new tactic of tying aid directly to inputs and 'desirable' techniques met with immediate success. The number of cattle which had been slowly declining since 1950 rose sharply in 1954 and went on rising thereafter. Expenditure on fertilizers which over the previous ten years had risen gradually from £27 million to £54 million jumped to £70 million in 1952–3. (A statistical analysis of the effects of some of these manipulations of input prices is contained in Cowling, Metcalf and Rayner (1970).[4] Changes in fertilizer prices relative to product prices appeared to have a highly significant effect on fertilizer use, though the authors do not discriminate between changes in fertilizer selling price and changes in effective price brought about by changes in the level of subsidy. Farmers are similarly shown to be highly sensitive to the grants that became available in the 1950s for the purchase of machinery.) The acreage of temporary grass, which had remained static between 1946 and 1950, began to rise and by the end of the 1950s showed an expansion of more than 20 per cent. Thus these two aspects of agricultural change, which have had serious environmental consequences, far from being simply an inevitable feature of 'progress', can be related directly to policy changes that occurred in the early 1950s. This is not to argue that they were caused by the policy developments alone. The whole battery of weapons at the Ministry of Agriculture's command, from the newly established National Agricultural Advisory Service to the manipulation of output prices, was used consistently to reinforce and push further changes that market forces were already encouraging; and ignore considerations market forces were anyway incapable of reflecting.

During the 1950s successive reviews extended the range and increased the value of production grants. One of the most significant additional grants covered a third of the cost of investment in permanent fixed equipment and long-term 'improvements' to land, such as hedgerow removal and land drainage schemes. The total value of all the grants was more than £100 million a year by 1960–1 when they accounted for nearly 40 per cent of all exchequer payments to farmers. They had also come to be used not only as a means of changing farming techniques and encouraging specific crops (field beans had a specific subsidy for a decade or more) but of directing aid to specific areas of the country.

It has been argued that the desire for equity for farmers' incomes *vis-à-vis* those of the rest of the community was one of the reasons underlying post-war agricultural support, but of course one of the inconsistencies of any price support scheme is that the richer the farmer, the more, in absolute terms, he benefits from the support. The production grants allowed aid to be directed with the accuracy at least of buckshot. By tying a number of grants to upland areas, some additional aid could be aimed in the general direction of the most needy. In upland areas farms tended to be smaller and the land less productive so farm incomes correspondingly lagged behind those of lowland farmers. A series of grants such as that on hill land ploughing (£12 per acre compared to £7 in lowland areas), on hill cows and hill sheep, bracken eradication and winter keep were introduced, spreading the erosion of countryside amenity to upland Britain. The loss of a large part of Exmoor to subsidy-induced intensive agriculture is perhaps the best-known example.

Under a new name these production grants persist even now. Although in title phased out by Britain's adoption of the CAP in the 1970s, it really worked the other way. The EEC adopted British production grants but called them the Farm Capital Grant Schemes.

In terms of marketable output – the only measure in which the Ministry of Agriculture has any interest – the policies of the early 1950s were a success. By the harvest year 1953–4 output was estimated to be 56 per cent above pre-war averages compared to the target increase of 60 per cent. But with world food prices continuing to fall, the resource costs of the policy were beginning to cause concern.

> In future home agriculture cannot be asked to produce a given amount of a commodity irrespective of cost. . . . It is evident that home agriculture cannot be completely insulated from world market conditions . . . [so] account must be taken of long term trends in market prices. The present cost to the taxpayer of the support given to British agriculture is very high – of the order of £200 millions [a figure to be exceeded the following and every succeeding year]. (Annual Review and Determination of Guarantees, 1954)

This 1954 Review marked two changes in the aims of policy. First, that output expansion should from now on be selective instead of across the board and, second, that there should be at least some concern with the efficiency of resource use in agriculture, although this concept of 'efficiency' was still not adequately defined. The commodities where expansion was still wanted included beef and home produced animal feedstuffs; those where further expansion was to be discouraged included pig meat, milk and wheat.

Successive Reviews throughout the 1950s stated successive ministers' determination not to increase the production of pig meat and milk. But while by the end of the decade the guaranteed pig-meat price had been reduced by 20 per cent, that of milk was not reduced at all. Partly encouraged by the financial inducements lavished on beef production, by 1961 milk output showed a 327 million gallon increase compared to a rise of only 26 million gallons in liquid milk consumption. This led to a situation summarized by Professor Nash:

> [Farmers] have . . . been urged to reduce their costs and make no further additions to the output of milk. But since the govern-

ment has continued to pay them handsomely for disregarding its advice it has inevitably created the impression either that it does not mean what it is saying or that it does not know what it is doing.[5]

In part the failure to reduce prices for products other than pig meat reflected the operation of the ratchet principle referred to on p. 66; governments find it easy to give aid but hard to take it away. But producers were in very different situations. Pig producers with the help of capital grants were rapidly taking advantage of new intensive techniques which, as with chickens, allowed economies of scale to be achieved without restructuring farm sizes. In the case of milk producers the structure was quite different. Just as supermarkets and street-corner sweet shops have different ideas about acceptable levels of profitability, so too do farmers. Milk production used notoriously to be the resort of the relatively small farmer lacking capital and other resources because, unlike crops, it yielded a monthly cheque and did not need very much equipment. On the grounds of equity these might be the farmers whom one would least like to squeeze, but almost certainly they would accept relatively low levels of return and if price manipulation was the instrument used to regulate production then it could not be used half-heartedly. Furthermore, being small, there were many of them, which gave them a certain political leverage, as we can still see today in the structure of the CAP. Thus because of their political power in the farming lobby – and perhaps too on equity grounds – the government found it especially hard to cut guaranteed milk prices. They relied on rising production costs gradually squeezing the profitability of production. But whilst it did this, because of the structure of producers (and the aid for beef) they accepted lower unit profits and reacted by producing even more milk to maintain their incomes. By 1957, foreshadowing the present crisis in CAP, the government was warning:

> Supplies [of milk] for manufacture, produced at considerable expense in terms of imported feed, now threaten to exceed the available manufacturing capacity at the peak period, while abundant supplies of milk products are available from Commonwealth countries which are particularly suited to the production of these commodities.[6]

In that same year the guaranteed price of milk was actually increased. The concern for efficiency in the broader sense of considering the best use of national resources, suggested in the 1954 Review, produced little except a minor dip in the growth of farmers' real incomes and was gradually replaced by the farming community's (and in this we include the Ministry of Agriculture) doggerel chant of labour productivity.

Another change in the early 1950s that must be noted in this review of policy was the introduction of so called 'deficiency payments'. Prior to 1953 first Labour and then, from 1951, Conservative governments had relied on the continuation of wartime controls. Farmers were paid directly by the government a fixed price for their produce.

In 1953 the Conservative government tried to reintroduce the institutions and forms of a free market whilst maintaining a system which allowed farmers to realize a bigger return than they could have got from selling on a free market. This 'decontrol' was implemented by means of the 'deficiency payments' scheme which was introduced for cereals in 1953. This worked by offering a guaranteed minimum price but allowing farmers to sell their produce on a free market. A deficiency payment was then made, calculated on the difference between the *average* price realized by, say, wheat during the year and the guaranteed price for wheat. If, for example, the guaranteed price for wheat was £1.49$\frac{1}{2}$p, per cwt, and the average price realized was £1.15p, then a payment of £0.34$\frac{1}{2}$p per cwt sold would be made to the farmer. This 'deficiency payment' would be made regardless of whether the farmer had actually sold his wheat for £1.10p, or £1.20p, a cwt. This was in order to retain a financial inducement to farmers to spread their sales according to market requirements as reflected in prices. The system of support via deficiency payments, which has the advantages of retaining some of the financial incentives to efficiency of a market system and also the favourable effects on income distribution that result from providing subsidies out of taxation rather than artificially high food prices, lasted right up to the enforced adoption of the EEC system in the early 1970s. It had little, however, to do with restoring a free market in agricultural produce.

The other notable policy development of the 1950s was the introduction in 1956 of 'long-term assurances' whereby the government restricted its powers to change the level of guaranteed prices. It agreed to keep the total value of its guarantees to farmers (broadly speaking the guaranteed price multiplied by the standard quantity applying to that commodity) at 97.5 per cent of the previous year, after taking account of the changes in costs that had taken place. This was undertaken in order to help farmers with their forward planning of production. (The standard quantity arrangements were first introduced for milk in 1954. At each Review the government announced a 'standard quantity' for output of particular commodities. If output then exceeded this figure the deficiency payments were calculated on the 'standard quantity' rather than on actual output. The 'standard quantity' mechanisms thus provided a means of imposing a ceiling on total subsidy for any commodity to which it was applied.)

Apart from the farm investment and 'improvement' scheme already referred to, the only other new policy of the 1950s aimed at encouraging 'efficiency' was introduced in 1958. This was the Small Farmer Assistance Scheme. It was supposed to help the small farmer, with a viable holding of between 20 and 100 acres but unable to finance his own improvements. Up to £6 per acre was to be available for modernization as well as further special aid for specific items such as ploughing permanent grass, ditching and land reclamation. All grants under the Small Farmer Scheme were additional to existing grants and brought gross assistance up to 85 per cent of the total cost of some projects.

Limitation of imports

The Small Farmers' Scheme, however, can be seen as the final development of the policy of encouraging 'efficiency' and weaning farmers from their subsidies. The new departure of the 1960s, as so often happens, did not result from any radical re-think on the part of policymakers but rather as a forced reaction to outside events which made eventual competitiveness and a 'reduction in the cost to the Exchequer' seem impossible. Under existing arrangements the Exchequer liability to farmers was jointly determined by the level of guaranteed prices and the level of world prices. The higher were world market prices then the closer they approached our own farmers' guaranteed prices and the less the Treasury had to pay out. But 1961–2 saw a precipitous fall in world prices for primary produce. Even if they had wanted to, the long-term assurances meant that the government could not lower United Kingdom internal prices in line with world prices, so the cost of implementing the guaranteed prices rose in one year from £151.2 million (1960–1) to £225.3 million (1961–2).

Falling world prices meant that one of two courses of action had to be taken. Either there had to be drastic action to reduce the level of agricultural support and restructure the industry or there had to be a tacit admission that there was no realistic hope of ever getting British agriculture to be competitive and a way found of limiting the absolute sum from public funds. Since the first course was ruled out by the power of the agricultural lobby and the recent long-term assurances entered into, the latter course was chosen. This was an admission that the declared aim of a self-supporting British agriculture was abandoned, but it had an offsetting subsidiary attraction to policymakers. The desire to enter the Common Market, which anyway entailed a long-term commitment to protected agriculture, suggested that it might be a good idea to couple the limitation of the Exchequer liability with some system more closely approximating to that of the EEC, with its levies on imported food.

There sprang from these events a fundamental change in the nature of the British market; though as is so often the British case, the fundamental change in position ultimately amounted to little more than a positional change of the fundament on our fence. From having leaned in the direction of totally free access for all agricultural goods to our home market we now leaned in the direction of import restriction. Before the changes of the early 1960s, though in name there was free access, in fact there were considerable restrictions; all horticultural protection came via tariffs, tariffs that in some cases were almost prohibitive. And many other goods, especially from non-Commonwealth sources, were subject to moderate tariffs. After the change we had moved further in the direction of restriction but compared to many other countries our barriers to imports remained low.

The new policy was to negotiate a series of gentlemen's agreements for individual commodities with our main suppliers limiting the quantity that could be sent and sometimes the minimum price at which it would be sold. The bacon agreement, more correctly known as the 'Bacon Market Sharing Understanding', aimed at controlling internal United Kingdom bacon prices, is a good example. In the convoluted words of the Ministry of Agriculture:

> Under the Understanding the United Kingdom determines annually a total minimum quantity for supplies to the United Kingdom market and a reserve quantity and allocates shares of the total minimum quantity between each of our main overseas suppliers and our own industry. HMG is obliged to use its best endeavours to keep United Kingdom production of bacon at the minimum allocation . . . the other participants . . . accept a similar obligation in respect of their exports to the UK market . . . allocations from the reserve may be made . . . as necessary to satisfy demand while maintaining stable prices at a reasonable level.[7]

These words are almost worthy of a Ministry of Truth. Since the participants accept an obligation to keep supplies to the minimum, the minimum is in fact a maximum.

In plain English, this means that the agreement restricted the total amount of bacon coming onto the United Kingdom market in order to keep up the price and stop the Treasury having to fork out too much money to farmers. Instead the money was forked out by bacon buyers via higher prices; higher prices which benefited not only our farmers but also overseas farmers participating in the restriction of supply. The Understanding does not reveal to whom the price level has to appear 'reasonable'.

Similar arrangements were negotiated for other commodities. In the same year a minimum import price agreement was negotiated for cereals, designed to stop imports of wheat or barley coming in at low prices. If world prices fell below the agreed minimum level then we were to impose levies to bring the price up to the minimum.

The first of these commodity agreements, however, discounting the Commonwealth Sugar agreement of 1950, was that for butter, reached in 1962. This regulated the quantity of butter coming into the United Kingdom and so controlled the price at which butter from any source was sold. This unplugged a convenient drain down which the growing surplus of milk production over liquid consumption could be poured. Home-produced milk for butter production, though it fluctuated from year to year, increased overall by some 50 per cent between 1959–60 and 1969–70. This agreement was also designed, however, to bolster New Zealand's earnings and as a precautionary dam against the already visible flood of surplus EEC butter.

Although designed to reduce farmers' claims on the Treasury by passing on part of the bill to the consumer and also, incidentally, to approximate slightly more closely to the Common Market's arrangements for protection, the 'success' of these commodity agreements cannot be simply judged in terms of how far the Exchequer's liabilities were cut. The cost of deficiency payments was reduced from £255.5 million in 1961–2 to £121.7 million in 1965–6, despite a small increase in the overall level of guaranteed prices, but a good part of this reduction resulted from higher world prices rather than higher prices on the United Kingdom market caused by our efforts to restrict incoming supplies. But certainly the commodity agreements were one factor. The policy changes of the early 1960s increased farmers' real incomes.

The pressure for expansion

In the later 1960s and through to the 1970s there was a further shift in the tone of policy. In response to growing pressure from the agricultural lobby there was a move, at first tentative and then more obvious and finally decisive, towards a more forceful and less selective expansion of home output with the attendant subsidies and environmental effects. The chronic balance of payments deficits and economic insecurity of this period provided this lobby with its opening.

The first echo of this new shift in emphasis can be found in the *National Plan*[8] introduced by the recently returned Labour government in 1965:

> Agriculture's main contribution to the Plan will be of two kinds. First, it will help through increased production to meet the growth in demand. This will ease the pressure on our bill for imports of temperate agricultural produce. (*National Plan*, 1965, Chapter 13)

But the *National Plan* did at least recognize that 'these develop-ments in agriculture had not been achieved without substantial cost and this must be taken into account in assessing the net gain to the national economy', even if it did conclude by recommending 'a further selective expansion programme'.

The report of the Economic Development Committee for Agriculture,[9] published three years later, did not attempt to discuss the pros and cons of alternative policies for agricultural expansion but started out by simply studying how much expansion was technically feasible. The report concluded that considerable expansion was possible given enough support and therefore, the chain of logic appears to have run, since it was technically feasible so it was desirable. No estimate of exactly what extra support would be necessary to achieve the increased output was given. The conclusion was that £220 million per annum of imports could be saved by the expansion; since it was difficult to estimate how much this would actually save, net, on the balance of payments, the EDC ignored the problem. (The reasons for this difficulty are discussed in Chapter 7.)

Even more strident advocacy of agricultural expansion came from the House of Commons Select Committee on Agriculture, whose report[10] was published in 1969. This committee, though overwhelmed with detailed and expert evidence, seemed to proceed on the basis of what you don't know, ignore. The evidence on such crucial matters as the costs of extra support, the net effect on the balance of payments, the cost in terms of resources and the returns the necessary resources would earn in alternative uses, were all dismissed as mere 'speculation'.[11]

This allowed the committee happily to reach the conclusion that 'it is desirable that expansion which has hitherto been intended to keep pace with the major part of the increase of home demand should go further and aim at a positive substitution of home-grown food for part of the present imports of temperate food-stuffs', and that this would be technically possible, provided the government 'provided adequate incentives', 'cut the rate of outflow of labour from agriculture' and ceased to allow rigid provisions in international agreements which offered some of the British market to overseas suppliers 'to inhibit domestic agricultural expansion'.

It is sometimes suggested that Britain has a Minister *for* rather than *of* Agriculture. One can say with more confidence that the Parliamentary Select Committee was *for* rather than *on* Agriculture. No less than 10 of the committee's 25 members were farmers; 2 more members belonged to other sections of the industry. Between them these 12 accounted for over 60 per cent of the total man-day attendances.

The culmination of this growing pressure came eventually in 1975. In that year a government White Paper, *Food from Our Own Resources*,[12] was published which established as official orthodoxy the special pleadings of the agricultural lobby. Indeed, on the question of the technical feasibility of expansion the government's White Paper simply took on board the NFU's estimates.[13]

To understand this change of official view – the government had shown little response to the growing pressures of the 1960s and had been positively brusque with the Select Committee on Agriculture – one must see the 1975 White Paper in the context of the early 1970s. Apart from entering the EEC and adopting CAP there was another factor. Between 1972 and 1974 there had been a sharp increase both relatively and absolutely in world prices of food and other raw materials, led by oil. In the 20 years from 1950, the cost of imported food relative to manufactured exports had been on average more or less constant. Then in two years the relative price of food imports leaped. Some observers, their Malthusian fears fuelled by the Club of Rome and other soothsayers of calamity, saw this not only as a change of level but as a continuing, perhaps accelerating, trend. In fact, as events have shown, the change was short-lived. By 1978 the world price of wheat, one of the leading temperate foodstuffs for which expansion was planned, had fallen to about half its peak level. Food prices relative to those of manufactured goods had fallen back sharply. Although this, too, may be temporary, few detached observers expect substantial relative increases in world food prices in the foreseeable future. Thus the whole basis of the White Paper's calculations of the viability of expansion, which in any case were not spelled out for assessment, appear, with hindsight, to be invalid. Nevertheless, the White Paper conceded a point which once conceded became established wisdom, gaining authority with every repetition. Even the environmental lobby took on board the expansion and implied intensification of British agriculture as a datum line in its calculations, as witnessed by the Nature Conservancy Council.[14]

This completes our survey of the development of purely British agricultural policy. It is a story of the growing influence of the agricultural lobby which by a process of political pressure group politics had come to dominate agricultural policy formation. This success has not surprisingly coincided with the transformation of the economic status of farmers and farming but also with the imposition of the narrow ideology of the farming community on that policy which, above all others, influences the pattern of the rural environment. That ideology, of course, is that the only appropriate use of land is to produce more food (for an already overfed nation) and that all obstacles to that end are impertinent interferences with the proper moral order of the world.

It is no coincidence that so many of our national leaders are now farmers. Successful politicians of both Conservative and Labour parties now own farms as a hallmark of their success; as do businessmen. Ownership of land as opposed to the workaday business of farming has for centuries been the most prestigious and acceptable form of social display in Britain. The wholesale movement out of industry into rural estates of the pioneer families of the Industrial Revolution is well documented and tended to coincide with periods of both agricultural and economic prosperity such as the first decade of the nineteenth century.[15] Perhaps the success of the farming lobby since 1940 and the interconnected growth in social prestige and economic rewards of being a farmer have established an equivalent movement for a slightly more egalitarian age. Now, instead of buying a 5000-acre estate, our Prime Ministers content themselves with 300-acre farms. But they are financially encouraged to do so by a maze of tax advantages and financial subsidies which the agricultural community has accumulated for itself in this century. In the concluding section of this chapter we document the effect these subsidies have had on farmers' incomes and on the price of agricultural land.

Changes in the relative economic position of farmers, 1938–77

Although, as was noted above, one of the primary aims of the 1947 Agriculture Act was to provide 'proper remuneration for farmers' and, ironically, for agricultural workers too, no estimates of individual farmers' average incomes have ever been produced.

This is especially remarkable given two further factors: that one of the most frequently advanced reasons for agricultural support (see Chapter 7) is that of equity, and that farmers' incomes are unfairly low compared to the rest of the community's; and, second, the fact that agriculture is statistically better documented – it has a whole Ministry to itself – than any other single industry.

The claims for support based on equity have almost always resorted to anecdotal evidence and to special cases; not to a systematic study of farmers' incomes, the distribution of incomes within the farming community and farm incomes relative to other groups in society. It is the function of this section to go at least some way towards remedying this.

There is available an income series for a sample of 2250 farms in England and Wales but, apart from excluding farmers in Scotland and Northern Ireland, there must be some doubt as to their reliability and the findings are not widely broadcast. These are shown in column two of Table 4.1, converted to constant 1976 prices and then shown as a ratio to mean wages of male manual workers. In column one of the table we have estimates of farmers' net income in the United Kingdom derived from the official estimates of the net income of the 'national farm'. These figures, which are updated annually, include, as do the figures in column two, a return on so-called 'tenant's' capital; that is, the value of stock and machinery but not fixed capital assets such as land and buildings. In so far as farmers are freeholders, therefore, they substantially underestimate the real income of the farming community because they do not allow for the return on investment in land and buildings. Also, since there has been a very strong trend towards freeholding, the overall growth of mean incomes in the farming community is underestimated.

To convert these figures to mean income per farmer, one has to divide by the number of farms, making allowance for the number of multiple holdings that there are. Official estimates of the number of holdings are easily obtainable from the various agricultural censuses and *A Century of Agricultural Statistics*.[16] Estimating the number of multiple holdings is more difficult. Two approaches were used. First, the official censuses of population for 1931, 1951, 1961 and 1971 show the number of people classified as 'farmers'. (There is one further qualification to make. The exact definition changed between the various census dates. In 1931 there was a separate classification of farmer; in 1951 and 1961 this was extended to include farm managers; and in 1971 extended again to include market gardeners. Allowance has been made for these changes of definition.) Second, a sample survey by Harrison[17] provided an independent estimate of the extent of multiple holdings. Putting together these two sources suggested that for every 100 holdings over 5 acres, there were 89 farmers and the extent of multiple holdings had changed surprisingly little over the period as a whole. Nevertheless, since in as far as there has been a change it appears to be towards an increase in multiple holdings, our series again underestimates the growth in individual farmers' mean incomes.

Both because of the special tax privileges attached to agriculture and because of the general tax advantages that income generated in a proprietor business offers (the ability to offset against tax many items of expense common to the business and to personal consumption, e.g. running a car, the costs of a telephone, travel, etc.), and finally because of the untaxed income in kind which farmers enjoy, the estimates of gross money incomes of farmers again understate their real net incomes and their relative position compared to other groups.

Of the sources of underestimation listed, probably the exclusion of income derived from the ownership of fixed capital and the exclusion of income in kind are the most important. As is discussed in more detail below, the increase in the value of agricultural land has produced, and has been produced by, a substantial increase in the income derived from its ownership. Between 1938 and 1977, the value of agricultural land at current prices increased by a factor of 35; between the same dates, farmers' incomes increased by a factor of 49, agricultural workers' by a factor of 32 and male manual workers' by a factor of 21.

Because real incomes of all groups, but especially those of farmers, are liable to fluctuation from year to year (as the data show, this conventional wisdom is less true than the frequency of its repetition would suggest. Given price changes, other groups have experienced large short-term changes in real income. Civil Service employees, for example, suffered a substantial reduction at the beginning of the Second World War, just as farmers enjoyed a very substantial increase), for the most part Table 4.1 gives averages over three- or five-year periods. The figures for 1938 and

Table 4.1 Estimated real incomes of farmers and other occupational groups, 1938–77 (£ per annum at 1976 prices and relative to male manual workers) (all figures for UK except where stated)

year	farmers[1] UK estimated £ 1976	ratio to MM	farmers[1] survey: England and Wales £ 1976	ratio to MM	male manual[2] £ 1976	agricultural workers[3] £ 1976	ratio to MM	army captain[4] £ 1976	ratio to MM	university lecturer[5] £ 1976	ratio to MM	Civil Service administrative principal[6] £ 1976	ratio to MM	executive officer[7] £ 1976	ratio to MM
1938	1,177	0.803	...	...	1,466	774	0.528	4,721	3.220	4,363	2.976	8,290	5.655	2,945	2.009
1939	2,414	1.579	...	...	1,529	858	0.561	4,630	3.028	4,337	2.836	8,071	5.279	2,867	1.875
1940-4	3,573	1.916	5,975	3.204	1,865	1,002	0.537	3,611	1.936	3,529	1.892	6,582	3.529	2,236	1.199
1945-7	3,164	1.749	3,443	1.903	1,809	1,328	0.734	3,676	2.032	3,343	1.848	5,928	3.277	2,105	1.164
1948-52	3,826	2.079	4,975	2.704	1,840	1,300	0.707	4,055	2.204	3,474	1.888	5,345	2.905	2,036	1.107
1953-7	3,403	1.646	5,002	2.420	2,067	1,371	0.663	3,614	1.748	3,637	1.760	5,352	2.589	2,064	0.999
1958-62	3,569	1.525	5,564	2.378	2,340	1,520	0.650	4,216	1.802	4,366	1.867	6,373	2.724	2,381	1.018

1963–7	3,961	1.481	6,825	2.552	2,674	1,758	0.657	4,331	1.620	4,653	1.740	7,030	2.629	2,526	0.945
1968–72	4,904	1.579	8,066	2.597	3,106	2,068	0.666	4,652	1.498	5,589	1.799	7,416	2.388	2,681	0.863
1973–7	7,384	2.089	10,368[8]	2.934	3,534	2,630[8]	0.744	4,525	1.280	5,828	1.649	7,252	2.052	2,815	0.797

Sources: See text and notes.

1 See text for explanation.
2 Figures for UK derived from the *British Labour Statistics Historical Abstract*,[18] years from 1969 from *British Labour Statistics: Yearbook*.[19]
3 Derived from *A Century of Agricultural Statistics*;[4] and MAFF updates.
4 Derived from Ministry of Defence private communication to authors. The figures relate to the starting salary of a combatant captain, married with one child. For early years, basic allowance for servant, rations and lodging are included. From 1970, these were consolidated into the military salary. There existed, and still exist, other allowances, such as regimental and command pay, separation and disturbance allowances; most serving captains would have, and do, qualify for one or more of these allowances during their service.
5 Data supplied by Association of University Teachers; figure is mean of minimum and maximum of the lecturer's scale (the career grade) exclusive of London weighting.
6/7 Data from private communications from Civil Service Department and First Division Association; early years from *Hansard*, May 1960. Mean of minimum and maximum of salary scales; principal's inclusive of London weighting since most serve in London; executive officer's exclusive of London weighting.
8 Includes figure for 1977 liable to revision.
. . . Not available.

1939 for the UK are shown separately, however, since they are the only pre-war data available and it is probable that 1939 figures already show the war's influence. It is impossible to know precisely how representative the 1938 figure on incomes of farmers in the UK is, but the indications are that it is reasonably representative. Both the volume of output and the Agricultural Price Index for all products were higher in 1938 than in most years between 1930 and 1938, suggesting farmers' money incomes were higher in 1938 than in most years in the 1930s. Although the Retail Price Index was also rising from 1933, the rise was not large enough to have offset the increase in money income. The supposition that 1938 farm incomes were reasonably typical of those of the decade to that date is reinforced by the pattern of changes reported in agricultural land prices. After falling from their 1927 level of £27.4 per acre to £21.3 in 1928, they stayed at around that level, gradually climbing after 1932. No sustained upward movement took place till after 1940, however: the date by which the increase in farm incomes from 1938 to 1939 might be expected to be beginning to influence people's views about the profitability of farming. For those reasons, 1938 incomes are reported since they appear to be not unrepresentative of the general level of the 1930s. The 1939 figures probably reflect the initial effects of the war.

The subsequent periods are chosen first as representing the full war years, then the post-war years prior to the 1947 Agriculture Act taking effect. Subsequently, the periods are five-year averages, though they correspond approximately to periods chosen for the analysis of policy earlier in this chapter. First there is the period of rising farm incomes immediately following the 1947 Act; then the period during the mid-1950s when the Conservative government was trying to reduce the dependence of agriculture on support; there follow four five-year periods of continuously rising incomes for farmers, first as the Conservative government retreated from their earlier positions and then during the 1960s and early 1970s as new forms of support, such as minimum price agreements and import controls, were introduced and world food prices recovered from their early 1960 lows. Finally there is the period of the mid-1970s, a time of unequalled prosperity, resulting from adaptation to the CAP and the boom in world primary product prices in the early 1970s.

The transformation of farmers' status both absolutely and relative to other groups is immediately apparent both from Table 4.1 and Figure 4.4, which is based upon the table. First, there was the recovery from the depression to the end of the war; that increased farmers' real incomes over the UK as a whole by a factor of about 3. Relative to male manual workers, their incomes did not rise to quite such an extent, though farmers did go from a mean income level rather below that of male manual workers to a level almost twice that of male manual workers.

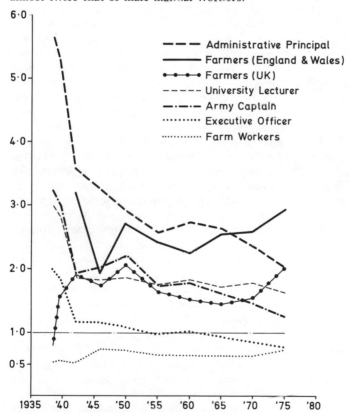

Figure 4.4   Incomes of farmers and other occupational groups relative to male manual workers, 1938–77

Source: As for Table 4.1 p. 83.

Farm workers over the same period did not improve their relative position and their absolute real income increased by an average of only £400 (in 1976 prices). All other occupational groups shown, representing white-collar middle-class occupations, suffered an absolute decline in real incomes and a substantial decline in their position relative to male manuals. The table also includes the survey estimates of farmers' mean incomes in England and Wales alone. This group, since it excludes the small, poor farmers of Northern Ireland and the lower income farmers in Scotland, has throughout the period had substantially larger incomes. With the exception of the immediate post-war years which included 1947, a drought year in which arable farmers did relatively badly, farmers in England and Wales compared to farmers throughout the UK have had mean incomes about half as high again. The difference is explained both by larger average farm sizes, in England especially, and by higher output. The general movements, however, are similar.

Looking at the period as a whole, we see farmers starting as, on average, a relatively poor group; then, with minor setbacks immediately after the Second World War was over, and again in the 1950s, they continuously improve their position. By the mid-1970s, farmers, even taking the UK as a whole, had the highest mean incomes of any group for which data are given. The mandarins of the Civil Service, the career grade Administrative Principals, had slowly slipped from earning over $5\frac{1}{2}$ times as much as the mean male manual wage (and over 7 times as much as the average farmer) to earning less than the average farmer and not much more than twice the male manual worker's wage. The position of the other traditional middle-class occupational groups shown in Table 4.1 had, in general, worsened in a similar way, though not from the same high level. Agricultural workers, who improved their relative position quite sharply just after the war, remained on a plateau and showed no further improvement, though farmers' incomes continued to surge ahead.

Thus the data fully support the assertions made in Chapter 4 and the arguments of Chapter 7 and elsewhere in this book. Looking at long-term trends, farmers, as a group, have moved from a position of absolute and relative poverty to a position of substantial prosperity. Since the estimates in Table 4.1 under-estimate rather than overestimate both farmers' incomes and the real value of those incomes, the degree of their prosperity is certainly even greater than the figures suggest. Furthermore, since it is reasonable to assume that incomes are distributed between farmers in a similar way to that in which output is produced, there will be a relatively large number of farmers with incomes below the mean and a smaller number of farmers with very high incomes indeed. Yet policy raises the incomes of rich farmers (who produce more output) by an amount almost directionally proportional to their richness.

Table 4.2 Land prices in England and Wales

year	price of agricultural land per acre (£1976)
1938	226.9
1939	218.3
1940–4	237.4
1945–7	224.1
1948–52	232.2
1953–7	215.3
1958–62	263.7
1963–7	414.6
1968–72	424.2
1973–7	680.1

Source: MAFF statistics, J. T. Ward[20] (1953).

Table 4.2 shows how the real price of agricultural land has changed since 1938. Although there was some increase during the war, no sustained increase came about until subsidies to farmers were well-established. From the late 1950s onwards, abstracting from short-run fluctuations there has been an increase in farm land prices which has gone on right to the end of the 1970s, although the figures in the table stop short in 1977. The tripling of land prices since the 1950s demonstrates a normal market reaction to the high level of agricultural subsidies. The acceleration in the 1970s reflected both the prospects of even higher support levels flowing from the CAP and the general movement of assets into real property following the acceleration of inflation in the 1960s.

Notes

1 Ricardo, D. (1817) *The Principles of Political Economy and Taxation*, chapter on Rent, London, John Murray.
2 Blythe, R. (1969) *Akenfield: Portrait of an English Village*, New York, Pantheon Books.
3 Addison, Lord C. (1939) *A Policy for British Agriculture*, London, Gollancz.
4 Cowling, K., Metcalf, D. and Rayner, A. J. (1970) *Resource Structure of British Agriculture: An Economic Analysis*, Oxford, Pergamon Press.
5 Nash, E. F. (1965) 'A Policy for Agriculture', in McCrone, G. and Attwood, A. E. (eds) *Agricultural Policy in Britain: Selected Papers by E. F. Nash*, Cardiff, University of Wales Press.
6 Annual Review and Determination of Guarantees (1957) Cmnd 109, London, HMSO.
7 House of Commons, Select Committee on Agriculture (1969) *Report and Evidence* London, HMSO, p. 68.
8 *National Plan* (1965) Cmnd 2764, London, HMSO.
9 Economic Development Committee for Agriculture (1968) *Agriculture's Import Saving Role*, London, HMSO.
10 House of Commons, Select Committee on Agriculture (1969), op. cit.
11 ibid., para. 13.
12 *Food from Our Own Resources* (1975) Cmnd 6020, London, HMSO.
13 ibid., para. 21.
14 Nature Conservancy Council (1977) *Nature Conservation and Agriculture*, London, HMSO.
15 Jones, E. L. (1967) 'Industrial capital and landed investment: the Arkwrights in Herefordshire, 1809–43', in Jones, E.L. and Mingay, G.E. (eds), *Land, Labour, and Population in the Industrial Revolution: Essays Presented to J. D. Chambers*, London, Edward Arnold.
16 Ministry of Agriculture, Fisheries and Food (1968) *A Century of Agricultural Statistics*, London, HMSO.
17 Harrison, A. (1975) *Farmers and Farm Businesses in England*, University of Reading, Department of Agricultural Economics and Management Miscellaneous Study no. 62.
18 *British Labour Statistics: Historical Abstract 1886–1968* (1971) London, HMSO.
19 *British Labour Statistics: Yearbook*, London, HMSO, annual.
20 Ward, J. T. (1953) 'Changes in the value of farm real estate in England and Wales, 1937–9 to 1951', *Farm Economist*, vol. VII, no. 4, Table 4.

5

The CAP regime

As it became increasingly obvious that Britain would enter the EEC, the policymakers began to clear the decks for CAP (the Common Agricultural Policy). Following the election of Mr Heath's Conservative government in 1970, the 1971 Annual Review set out the new policy:

> The Government's declared aim is to adapt the present system of agricultural support to one relying increasingly on import levy arrangements, under which the farmer will get his return increasingly from the market. (Annual Review and Determination of Guarantees, 1971)

This process meant that the burden of agricultural support was to be largely transferred from citizens as taxpayers to citizens as buyers of food. Although the tax structure as a whole is not on balance especially progressive, expenditure on food falls sharply as a proportion of household budgets, as families get richer. Thus the proposed transfer was sharply regressive in terms of its effects on the distribution of income in society as a whole, more especially so since in Britain, unlike the Continent, the average farmer was already clearly in the very richest segment of society, as the previous chapter demonstrates. But that it was part of a continuous process rather than a revolutionary change should be apparent from the previous discussion of the development of import restrictions in the 1960s. Apart from its regressive effects on income distribution, the change merely relieved the Exchequer of most of its highly visible payments to farmers at the cost of raising food prices and, as it turned out, of expanding yet further the proportionate share of expensive domestic production in total food consumption.

The reasons for this last feature were threefold. As is discussed below in more detail, the average level of support under CAP, which we were shortly to join, was higher than that previously ruling in Britain. In any event, a given level of support via levies on imports will tend to induce an expansion of the share of domestic output compared to the same level of support offered via deficiency payments since the higher prices tend to choke off domestic demand but not, of course, supply. Finally, after entry, especially given the extent to which EEC revenues were dependent on levies on imports of food from third countries, it came to be argued, oversimplistically, that expansion of domestic output was necessary to reduce British net contributions to central EEC funds.

The determining reason for the phasing out of the deficiency payments system was the over-riding aim of Mr Heath's Conservative government to gain entry to the EEC. There were, however, a number of subsidiary reasons. The Conservative party has a traditional hostility to government spending and although it changed nothing real, the move to import levies could be presented as a reduction in government spending. This particularly found favour with farmers. Exchequer support of agriculture has the objective advantage that it is clearly visible and quantifiable. This makes informed public discussion and criticism of policy easier. Import levies mean that price support becomes 'invisible' and hard to quantify precisely; so informed public discussion becomes more difficult and criticism gets directed to relative side issues such as butter mountains rather than the real costs to the community of the policy. Around 1970, the phrase 'farmers will get their return from the market'[1] was extremely popular with farmers. Very few pointed out that the market prices from which they would get their return would be wholly controlled by public intervention and bear no relation to world market prices.

As has already been indicated, the basic method of agricultural support under CAP is controlled consumer prices, organized via levies on imports from third countries and, where necessary, via intervention buying. It is not our intention to explain the detailed mechanics of the system. Although in outline simple, the policy as it has developed has acquired a bureaucratic complexity of almost Kafkaesque proportions. The simplest and most accessible explanation of the outlines of CAP known to us was in *Money Which?*[2]

Here we will give just the briefest summary. Guaranteed prices, operational throughout the EEC but denominated in Units of Account (UAs), are agreed annually by the Council of Ministers; these in general are referred to as 'target' prices and are those on which farmers may be expected to make production plans. The mechanisms of CAP then prevent supplies reaching consumers at lower prices. Imports from lower cost external producers are subject to a variable levy set to raise prices to the 'threshold' prices (i.e. the target prices less transport costs from ports to centres of consumption). Any quantity of EEC production over and above that which consumers will buy at the target price is subject to 'intervention' buying at the 'intervention' price, which in general is some 93 per cent of the target price. These purchases of 'surplus' output may (i) be stored (the mountains and lakes of CAP) until they can be resold within the EEC without the price falling below the target. Since this almost never happens they are more usually (ii) exported, with the help of a subsidy to the exporter, to bring the price down to the world market level — except that blunt names such as 'export subsidies' are not used: the EEC jargon is a 'restitution payment' or 'export refund'. Alternatively, surpluses may be 'denatured', i.e. rendered unfit for human consumption, and sold for industrial purposes or for animal feeds. This is the mechanism which allows us to witness the absurd and shameful spectacle of excess milk (and even butter) production, induced by the high level of guaranteed prices, being used in compound feeds for cows to produce yet more surplus milk; though it must be acknowledged that it is more often skim milk for pig or calf feed.

A considerable complication in this system has arisen as a result of the instability in exchange rates that has become endemic for most countries, especially for Britain, since the late 1960s. CAP prices are denominated in terms of UAs but, of course, farmers are paid in their domestic currencies. There has, therefore, to be a rate of exchange between each member country's currency and the EEC's UA. If this were set in world currency markets or even determined by some automatic formula, this might not cause a very serious problem. But the rate is a 'representative' rate determined by member countries, the so-called 'green pound' and 'green franc'. Given the unanimity rule of the Council of Ministers which existed up to 1982, this has meant that any country, the value of whose currency on world markets would have indicated a devaluation or revaluation of their exchange rate with the UA, has had an effective veto; if the market value of its currency fell against the UA, implying a devaluation of its representative rate, it could refuse. Naturally member countries have tended to be guided by their self-interest as they see it.

When the pound was falling against other currencies, for example during 1976, the 'green pound' rate with the UA was not adjusted downwards by the same proportion. Thus if a particular commodity's guaranteed price were, say, 100 UA a tonne, the 'green pound' rate was 2 UA to the £ and the 'green franc' rate was Fr5 to the UA, the British farmer would be getting £50 per tonne and his French equivalent Fr500. If the market rate of exchange was, and remained at, Fr10 to the £ there would be no problem. But with the instability in world exchange markets since 1970, serious problems have arisen. In periods such as 1976 the policy of the then Labour government not to devalue the 'green pound' to the extent of the fall in the value of the real pound produced significant benefits for the British consumer by keeping down food prices below the artificial level of the CAP. To return to our example above, if the real pound fell to only Fr8 but the 'green pound' stayed at a level of Fr10, then the French farmer would now be getting the equivalent of £62.5 per tonne whilst the British farmer continued to get £50.

Whilst this produced a benefit for the British consumer (though that is a very qualified statement – the price of food in Britain remained well above the world market price at which it would have been available to the British consumer without the CAP), it meant UK farmers were getting lower prices than the French. Consequently the French would not willingly export food to Britain and the British would have much preferred to sell the produce in France. To get round this problem the EEC invented yet another bureaucratic device, the 'monetary compensatory amounts' (MCAs) which were subsidies and levies raised on internal trade in food designed to equalize final selling prices in each member country. Apart from creating yet a further complication, the prospect of these MCAs produced a new form of fraud: circulating food or giving the appearance of circulating it by manipulating the appropriate pieces of paper, from country to country, collecting MCAs 'en route'.

This Labour party policy was totally reversed in 1980–1 by the new Conservative Minister of Agriculture, Peter Walker, himself a farmer. By 1980 the problem was not a falling £ but a rising one and what Peter Walker did was fail to increase the value of the green pound in line with the real £'s appreciation against other European countries. Thus in terms of our example above, the real £ went from Fr8 to Fr12 so the £50 per tonne the British farmer was getting became worth Fr600 compared to the French price of Fr500. We now had to levy MCAs on 'cheap' imports from the EEC over and above the CAP import levies, already inflating the price of food coming in from the rest of the world. As Samuel Brittan plaintively but inaccurately wrote: 'for the first time since the repeal of the Corn Laws there will be a tax on imported foodstuffs'.[3] Inaccurate, of course, because as we will see below the essence of CAP was a variable but generally very substantial tax on imported foodstuffs and we had been members since 1973. And anyway, on a limited range of foodstuffs, especially horticultural produce, there had been import taxes for many years. The point was that policy in 1980/1 was to place a tax on imported foodstuffs over and above the already extortionate tax levied by the dictates of CAP.

This brings us to the question of how much the CAP in fact costs. At the outset we would warn our readers that although we will provide an answer, no answer which is completely accurate, nor even an answer on which potential margins of error can be estimated, can be provided. We do not wish to claim accuracy for our answer; only that the figures we produce appear to us to be the best that can be done. For this we make no apology. As was remarked earlier in this chapter, we suspect one of the features of CAP that is attractive to both governments and farmers is that the form of subsidy is such that no clear estimate of its costs to consumers and taxpayers can be made. We regard this as a grave disservice to the citizens of Europe and an example of the politicians' sleight of hand which leads to their generally low rep·itation for probity. The problem of estimating the cost of CAP to the consumer, or its value to the farmer, is that whilst we can easily measure the direct costs, we cannot measure at all easily the great bulk of that iceberg of support which is hidden by eliminating cheaper imports. In any all-embracing estimate of the costs of agricultural support one would have to include two further types of cost: (i) supply side subsidies, both visible, such as farm capital grants, and invisible, such as the various tax advantages including rating relief and relief from fuel oil duties that agriculture enjoys but other economic activity does not; and (ii) the external costs of environmental damage about which this book is chiefly concerned.

The two most difficult problems encountered are first that of estimating the real world price of commodities at which they would be available to consumers in the absence of CAP and second the fact that the value of protection calculated is at best only valid for the particular period for which the calculation was done. Fluctuations in world product prices mean the value of CAP to farmers can vary hugely from year to year. Indeed in the exceptional years of 1973 and 1974, before the British system had been fully adjusted to CAP, the policy appears actually to have reduced some consumer prices in Europe below the level they would otherwise have been.

Even with 'simple' commodities such as cereals, where there is a well-established world market, there is the problem of deciding what that world price would be in the absence of protection. Whilst it may be reasonable to suppose that the world price would remain constant if protection were changed just very slightly, and not wholly unreasonable to make that assumption to calculate the value of support for just one country, it is plainly unreasonable to suppose that the world market price would not be changed by the cessation of all agricultural support in the EEC. The problem is that since any significant change in the level of support would within a year or so affect the level of production in the EEC, there would in turn be an induced change in world prices.

In the case of more complicated commodities such as milk and dairy products, the problem is made more difficult still by the virtual absence of a clear world market price for liquid milk. Transport costs and health regulations more or less eliminate trade in liquid milk on a world basis. Couple the absence of a world market price with the continued activities of the Milk Marketing Board, who maintain domestic prices by means of their monopoly powers over milk purchases and distribution, and the process becomes incapable of exact solution beyond reasonable dispute. The discrete action in such circumstances might be simply to enter the value of protection for milk as 'unknown' in Table 5.2. This would be misleading, however, since one fact of which we are certain is that protection for milk and milk products is very substantial indeed and the powers of the Milk Marketing Board have ensured that despite the already massive support of CAP for milk and milk products, liquid milk prices in Britain are generally the highest in the EEC.

Because there are established world market prices for milk products, such as butter and cheese, the level of import levies applied on imports of milk products provides a sound indicator of the level of protection CAP affords milk sold for manufacture. For the purposes of quantifying the effects of the Milk Marketing Board's monopoly, we have assumed that the price advantage it gives is equal to the margin of the liquid price over that of milk for processing into whole milk powder. We have then calculated three alternative measures of the overall value of protection for milk and milk products:

(i)   Protection for milk sold for manufacture only.
(ii)   Protection assuming all milk is protected at the same rate as the average for manufacturing.
(iii)   As (ii) plus estimate of the value of the monopoly on sales of liquid milk calculated as indicated in text.

This last procedure is in line with that adopted by Josling (1973) in his earlier estimates of the value of CAP for the late 1960s and early 1970s.[4]

Let us start with the simplest and most uncontroversial of figures, that for public expenditure in Britain (Northern Ireland is counted separately) on all forms of agricultural support. In the two financial years including 1979 this averaged £345.1 million or £1137 per farmer or £515 for every farmer and worker in agriculture. In 1980/1, with the return of a Conservative government committed to making industry stand on its own feet without government support or intervention, the estimated total was £567.6 million or £1918 per farmer, £872 per farmer and worker.

But, as was mentioned earlier, this visible support, because of the artificial prices induced by import levies and MCAs, is only the tip of an iceberg. Table 5.2, derived from a paper by Black and Bowers,[5] gives some more inclusive estimates of support for the main agricultural products. Though even these, since (following Josling[6]) they include only the support measures directly affecting demand, still omit many types of support. All types of agricultural support are classified in Table 5.1.

Table 5.1 The sources of support for British farmers under the CAP regime

source (included in Table 5.2 estimates)	comments
import levies	designed to bring import prices up to CAP levels; based on day-to-day monitoring of world market prices
Monetary Compensatory Amounts (MCAs)	designed to offset differences between actual exchange rates and 'green' rates
export subsidies (restitution payments)	designed to allow surplus expensive EEC produce to be sold on world markets at world prices
storage costs	cost of storing surplus produce
monopoly power of Milk Marketing Board	it is still the case that milk production must legally be sold through the Milk Marketing Board; by restricting supplies of liquid milk and eliminating imports even from other EEC countries, the domestic price in Britain is maintained well above the level that would otherwise prevail; for the purposes of the calculations in Table 5.2, it was assumed that the value of these monopoly powers was equal to the difference between the liquid milk price and that for powdered milk
direct production subsidies	the subsidy on hill cattle and sheep was included as direct and

specific; other, more generalized,
production subsidies were
excluded in the Table 5.2 estimates

source (excluded in Table 5.2 estimates)	comments
general production grants	these include expenditures under the various headings of the Fonds Europeen d'Orientation et de Garantie Agricole (FEOGA); there is, for example, a grant of up to 70% paid for any agricultural investment, e.g. for 'grassland regeneration', field drainage, etc.
'consumer' subsidies	there have been schemes designed to boost consumption of certain products, especially butter, notoriously in overproduction
de-rating of agricultural land	this has been the case since 1929 and gives agriculture a significant advantage *vis-à-vis* manufacturing and service industries; recent estimates for England and Wales range from around £320m in 1982/3* to £660m for 1980/1**
relief of fuel oil duty	agriculture is exempt from the duty on fuel oils which make up 35% of their price to industry and private consumers; this encourages the use of energy-intensive techniques in agriculture
capital transfer tax provisions	agricultural land enjoys a unique and preferential position with respect to capital transfer tax
research costs/farm advice	most research in agriculture and the advisory services that ensure that research results are acted on is publicly funded; MAFF is the chief source of these funds; its estimate is that their total value in 1981/2 was £149.3m***

health regulations	health regulations have been used on occasion to provide further back-door support for British farmers; a recent example was the decision to prohibit the import of poultry from countries that inoculated against fowl pest (instead of slaughtering, as is the practice in Britain); this was designed to keep out French turkeys

---

*   MAFF evidence to the House of Commons Agriculture Committee (1982) *1st Report from Agriculture Committee Session 1981–82, Minutes of Evidence, Appendix 15*, H.C.41-II. MAFF estimated a rateable value of £200m for agricultural land in England and Wales; to this has been applied the average rate poundage for the shire counties to produce the estimate of £320 for 1982/3.

**   Quoted in Coopers and Lybrand Associates Ltd., *Report on Non-Domestic Rates with Particular Reference to Small Firms*, report for Shell U.K. Ltd., London, 1980. The report recommended the re-rating of agricultural land.

*** *Minutes of Evidence 11th November 1982* to House of Commons Agriculture Committee. The 1981–2 figure represented an increase in real terms of 18.9 per cent on the total for 1977–8; this, at 1977–8 prices, was £77.2m.

Though subject to necessary cautions in interpretation, the estimates in Table 5.2 are conservative in that the assumptions tended systematically to be cautious rather than extreme; thus, for example, so-called 'consumer' subsidies, such as those on school milk and on butter, and non-product specific direct subsidies, plus the whole array of tax advantages farming enjoys, have been excluded. The figures, nevertheless, show clearly the enormous degree of support agriculture enjoys from the combination of CAP and the continuing national subsidies; a degree of support which has almost certainly increased sharply since Peter Walker took over as Minister of Agriculture.

For individual products, milk and milk products enjoy both the highest proportionate and the highest absolute degree of support, equivalent in 1979 to an average tariff of at least 160 per cent and more realistically 750 per cent. Reflecting this level of support, specialist dairy farming per acre yielded the highest net income in 1978/80. Nevertheless, cereals have been highly profitable. With a mean estimated adjusted nominal tariff equivalent of 60.6 per cent, they have enjoyed very considerable protection (the most recent estimates for manufacturing industry, by Kitchen,[7] show an upper limit of 21 per cent) and since their high priced output is an input into livestock and dairy farming, this raises the costs for other farmers. Thus we have a vicious circle of protection ensuring yet more protection, as dairy and livestock farmers lobby for higher product prices. This tends to produce an increase in target prices across the board, which in turn raises costs in dairy and livestock farming. The evidence of where surplus production is mainly concentrated, in milk products, does reinforce the view that dairying is the most outrageously protected area. Indeed further calculations by Black and Bowers[8] strongly suggest that the value of milk production, once you subtract protection, is below its real costs of production. At the margin, therefore, this protection is reducing real national income, not increasing it.

Producer Subsidy Equivalent tells us the proportion of the farmers' returns that came from support measures. As can be seen, only pig farmers in 1977 showed any sign of truly 'getting their returns from the market'. A more representative position would be that of wheat with about 35 to 40 per cent of the farmers' return coming from support measures. The most extreme case is provided by milk, where in 1979, from 0.5 to 97 per cent of the farmers' returns were from support measures. During most of the 1970s dairy products were not only in oversupply in the EEC (which, for example in 1976, had five-and-a-half years' supply of powdered milk in store) but in world markets generally. This kept world prices very low and so the costs of support commensurately high.

As is explained in the footnotes to Table 5.2, these calculations of CAP support are more properly interpreted as percentage support on the margin of production since implicit in them is the view that world prices would not change if the level of support did. Despite this caveat, we have, nevertheless, provided figures for the total value of support UK agriculture enjoyed in 1977/9. We do this since our judgement is that the order of magnitude is likely to be right and it is impossible to calculate a better figure.

Table 5.2 Measure of support for UK agriculture under CAP

product	producer subsidy equivalent %[1]			adjusted nominal tariff equivalent %[2]			total value £ millions[3]		
	1977	1978	1979	1977	1978	1979	1977	1978	1979
wheat	42.6	32.1	42.4	74.2	47.1	73.2	185.3	179.9	288.4
barley	21.5	39.9	46.5	27.3	60.9	80.7	174.2	304.9	396.3
sugar	39.4	54.9	71.0	64.9	119.7	226.3	52.4	87.3	146.3
potatoes[4]	15.9	24.1	18.7	18.5	28.4	22.0	59.7	60.9	70.0
beef	52.4	45.6	56.1	95.2	76.5	116.1	555.2	573.0	798.7
lamb[4]	25.1	23.2	33.6	29.7	27.9	40.3	67.1	69.7	107.1
pigmeat	1.6	8.1	23.2	1.6	8.8	30.2	10.5	55.8	172.8
milk i)[5]	46.7	40.5	50.2	141.6	117.7	163.1	693.5	655.3	883.5
ii)	83.9	71.3	88.9	322.3	214.3	471.2	1,244.6	1,154.3	1,566.1
iii)	93.8	80.5	96.7	490.2	283.9	756.8	1,392.6	1,303.6	1,702.4
total value lower[6]	£ million						1,797.9	1,986.8	2,863.1
upper[6]	£ million						2,497.0	2,635.1	3,682.0
total per farmer[6]	£						6,074	6,557	9,418
	£						8,436	8,697	12,112
total per farmer[6] and worker[6]	£						2,668	2,935	4,331
	£						3,705	3,892	5,570
total per hectare[6]	£						94.9	104.8	151.2
	£						131.2	139.0	194.4

per acre[6]	£			38.4	42.4	61.2
	£			53.3	56.3	78.7
as % of mean[6]				65.9	61.3	74.2
rent[6]				91.1	81.3	95.3

Source: Derived from Black and Bowers (1981), op. cit.

1 Producer Subsidy Equivalent is calculated as:

$\dfrac{(V^m + D - V^w)}{}$ where V^w = total value of domestic output in world market,

V^m = total value of domestic output at protected prices in home market

D = total value of direct subsidies

Thus Producer Subsidy Equivalent can be thought of as the proportion of the value the farmer receives that is made up by subsidies. Since if subsidies were withdrawn both output and domestic and world prices would change it is more reliable as a guide to the value of support to farmers at the margin than to the true value of total support. Thus if wheat output had, in 1979, been 100 tonnes greater, it is reasonable to assume some 40 per cent of the revenue received by farmers would have been by way of support from the rest of the community. The estimates of the total value of support must therefore be interpreted with this qualification in mind.

2 Adjusted nominal equivalent tariff is calculated as: $\dfrac{(V^m + D - V^w)}{V^m}$ and can therefore be thought of as the percentage tariff that would have to be put on imports to yield the same overall protection.

3 Total value of support is subject to the qualification indicated above.

4 Potatoes are not yet subject to protection under CAP, only to national support measures. Arrangements for lamb were not arrived at until October 1980.

5 Calculated in the three ways indicated in the text.

6 The lower total is on the basis of the lowest estimate for milk subsidies, viz. protection only for milk sold for manufacturing; the highest estimate is that including a value for the monopoly of the Milk Marketing Board assuming that to be worth the difference between the liquid milk price and the price realized for milk to be processed into powder.

In 1979 it appears that support was worth about £10,000 per farmer or £5000 per farmer plus worker in the industry. Another way of looking at it, particularly relevant for the argument of this book, is per unit area. Our argument is that the level and type of agricultural support has had a highly significant effect on the type and intensity of farming and hence on the rural environment. Society has been subsidizing the degradation of the countryside. Econometric evidence, for example, that of Cowling, Metcalf and Rayner,[9] suggests that farmers are as close to being 'economic' men as can readily be found and respond predictably and significantly to relative cost and price changes. In ignorance of this, laymen may think that farmers do not respond to perceived prices very readily; it may be thought, for example, that agricultural change is the result of some disembodied and unstoppable 'technical progress'. But the level of support provided for agriculture per unit area is somewhere between 60 and 95 per cent of the level of average rents. In 1979 farmers were getting something between £60 and £80 for every acre of the UK under agriculture and very much more in lowland Britain since all the upland rough grazing has been included in that calculation. Even at an intuitive level, it is not very convincing to suggest that financial leverage on such a scale would leave farming systems unmodified.

These estimates of the effective protection afforded farmers in the UK since our membership of CAP, relate only to the years for which they were compiled. We cannot conclude, therefore, that agricultural protection is necessarily greater than that for manu-facturing. The level of agricultural protection varies with world prices and, indeed, protection can be negative (i.e. prices to consumers can be lower than they would be if supplies came in at world market prices), as was the case for sugar during 1974–5. Some have concluded, therefore, that such calculations are futile. We do not take this view. It is clear, both from the design and intention of CAP and from the experience of operating it since 1967 when common prices were first introduced, that internal prices tend to be considerably in excess of those on world markets. The calculations here are illustrative of three of those years and, in our judgement, of the likely normality of CAP for the foreseeable future.

It should be borne in mind, however, that they relate only to the British market. Although the original intention was for prices to be uniform throughout Europe, this ceased to be the case within two years of CAP's introduction when the French, following their devaluation in 1969, refused to allow internal food prices to rise to the extent of the devaluation. Since then, national governments have had, via their control of 'green' exchange rates, partial control over internal food prices. In addition, some purely national support mechanisms have been retained. Thus CAP is not a common policy for Europe but a regime with a national interpretation.

There are many criticisms of CAP from a British viewpoint. When considering what is wrong with the policy, our conclusion was that it was difficult to discover anything that was right. In the academic literature criticisms have tended to become more esoteric and technical. But the basic facts are unavoidable. The policy is inequitable. Although when the original six EEC members established the policy, at the instigation of the French who nationally stood most to benefit, European farmers were indeed poor; in Britain, as we have already shown, the average farmer has been relatively rich since the Second World War. The average farmer is now decidedly rich both in terms of income and even more especially in terms of wealth. In 1979 an English freehold farmer with a quite modest holding of 75 hectares had, in land alone, assets worth £242,000; a substantial farmer with 350 hectares had assets in land of £1,130,000. Not only is the policy regressive in that it transfers real income from the relatively poor to the relatively rich, it is regressive within the farming community. Support is mainly on output, so the bigger the farmer is and, therefore, the richer, the greater volume of support he enjoys. Quite literally the policy is producing millionaires from the public purse.

The second great objection to CAP as far as Britain is concerned is that internationally it transfers resources from EEC countries which are net importers to those that are net exporters – which is why the French and the Irish, for example, benefit. Britain is not only inevitably a net importer of food but, as we hope we have demonstrated in this book, it is not in our interests, realistically, to be anything else. Britain could become self-sufficient in temperate food by becoming close to vegetarian. Whilst that might be good for our health, and perhaps our souls too, it is not likely to come about. Alternatively we can become more self-sufficient within the confines of CAP by an unsupportably high level of subsidy and a degree of agricultural intensity which will have ever more severe effects on the countryside and bring farmers into ever sharper conflict with the rest of the community.

Other criticisms of CAP relate to its impact on world markets. Because EEC prices do not vary with either internal or world supply and demand, they do not adjust to conditions of shortage or surplus. If there is a shortfall in world supplies of, say, wheat, somehow world consumption has to adjust. CAP ensures that that adjustment takes place outside Europe and since adjustment is occurring in a smaller total market, the necessary price increase outside the EEC will have to be larger. The more countries that adopt CAP-style protection, the greater the instability in world food prices that will arise and the more frantic will be the swings into apparent shortage and glut. Under the old deficiency payments system this tendency was much less marked since imports and domestic production sold at world prices, more or less, and so domestic consumption, if not production (since producers received a guaranteed price), responded to world supply and demand conditions.

There is even the probability under the CAP regime that British and European reactions to a world shortage of wheat would lead to increased EEC consumption of wheat and so further aggravate the problem. This is because (see Swinbank[10]) some products that are substitutes for wheat in uses such as animal foods, for example, soya beans and manioc, are not subject to import restrictions and enter at prices determined by world market conditions. A world shortage of wheat would cause substitution of soya meal for wheat in compound feeds outside the EEC, and so increase soya prices. This, in turn, would cause EEC animal feed compounders and farmers to feed more of the now relatively cheaper wheat to animals since wheat prices in the EEC would remain unchanged. This would then put further pressure on world wheat prices and even further increase price fluctuations on world markets.

There are still more criticisms of the effects of CAP on other countries. Apart from aggravating price fluctuations elsewhere, the CAP, because of its high levels of support, encourages surplus production. This tends to be dumped, sometimes in disguise as 'food aid', on other countries, especially at times of world surplus. Although developed countries, such as the USSR, may sometimes find that convenient as, too, may Third World countries suffering from some temporary calamitous food shortage, there are strong reasons for believing that, in general, a sudden short-term availability of surplus production at low prices is extremely disruptive for Third World countries trying to encourage the long-term development of a modern agriculture. The emerging farmers suddenly find that their incomes shrivel and their investment produces nothing and development plans are consequently disrupted.

These problems are intensified for Third World countries by the EEC practice of levying systematically higher import duties on processed goods. Thus oil seeds which do not compete with EEC production are allowed in free; crude vegetable oil for industrial purposes at 5 per cent or 10 per cent if for food; refined vegetable oil at 8 or 15 per cent; hardened vegetable oil at 17 per cent; and, finally, margarine imports are subject to an import duty of 25 per cent. This systematically handicaps developing countries in their attempts to encourage processing industries based on their local agriculture.

The CAP regime then stands condemned on grounds of equity; it is inequitable both within agriculture, within Britain, between Britain and richer EEC countries that are less dependent on imported food, and finally between the EEC and poorer countries. It is inefficient; it transfers resources to less productive use and, indeed, appears sometimes to divert resources to purposes (e.g. extra milk production) where they not only produce less than they could elsewhere but lose value absolutely.

Finally, and more importantly for our argument, CAP has the effect of subsidizing and intensifying activities and agricultural practices that greatly increase the net external costs of agriculture. The standard economic argument is that one reason for government intervention is to reduce external costs where they are important. This leads to one of the economic arguments for subsidizing public transport, that it reduces congestion which is an external cost, i.e. a cost not paid by those that produce it. Similarly, there is an economic argument for public support for producing certain types of goods, known as public goods, by government where their production by means of the market mechanism would be inefficient. The classic example is defence, though the road network or public parks are partial examples.

In the case of CAP we are spending very large sums of money and offering price protection to ensure the opposite. Goods that farmers produce that have effective market prices are highly subsidized. Goods, such as a beautiful countryside or a rich and healthy rural environment, that have no market prices, get no subsidy. We directly subsidize activities, e.g. drainage or the use of capital intensive techniques, that have external costs but offer quite nugatory support for practices that have environmental benefits. Most importantly of all, the overall level of support is such that the cost to the farmer of conservation becomes prohibitive and intensification the only route to financial survival. We have produced a system of agricultural support that has to it a through-the-looking-glass logic of totally inverting what would be economically and indeed socially desirable.

Notes

1 Jim Prior, then Minister of Agriculture, quoted in the *Guardian*, 22 October 1970.
2 'Common Agricultural Policy', *Money Which?*, June 1977, pp. 334–42.
3 *The Financial Times*, 8 April 1980.
4 Josling, T. J. *et al.* (1973) *Domestic Policy and International Trade*, Document C73/LIM/9, FAO, Rome.
5 Black, C. J. and Bowers, J. K. (1981) 'The level of protection of UK agriculture', University of Leeds, School of Economic Studies Discussion Paper no. 99.
6 Josling (1973), op. cit.
7 Kitchen, P. D. (1976) 'Effective rates of protection in UK manufacturing for 1963 and 1968', in Artis, M. J. and Nobay, A. R. (eds) *Essays in Economic Analysis*, Cambridge, Cambridge University Press.
8 Black and Bowers (1981), op. cit.
9 Cowling, K. G., Metcalf, D. and Rayner, A. J. (1970) *Resource Structure of Agriculture: an Economic Analysis*, Oxford, Pergamon Press.
10 Swinbank, A. (1980) 'European Community agriculture and the world market', *American Journal of Agricultural Economics*, vol. 62, no. 3.

6

Agriculture and economic efficiency

As was documented in Chapter 4, the post-war period has been one of considerable prosperity for British agriculture. An increase in the rate of growth of output and a substantial restructuring were achieved of necessity during the Second World War; the alternative to expansion of home agriculture being seen as, if not starvation, at least reduced nutritional standards. Strategic considerations and balance of payments difficulties led to a continuing commitment to agricultural expansion after the war. The nature of warfare changed and balance of payments problems came and went, but the commitment to expansion continued. The arguments for it are discussed in Chapter 4 and further in Chapter 7. The methods by which the expansion was achieved are outlined also in Chapter 4. The social and environmental consequences were discussed in Chapters 2 and 3. In this chapter we consider the extent of the expansion and the broad economic thinking that lay behind it.

If we value output at the prices farmers receive for their produce, then its total value, technically gross output at current prices, increased at a little less than 2.5 per cent per annum over the period 1954–68. Recently this growth has been much faster – over 12 per cent per annum between 1967 and 1977. This growth has been made up partly of increases in prices and partly of an increase

in output, with of course considerable variation in the com-
position of output. The economist is more interested in net than
gross output and in real changes rather than those which merely
reflect inflation. Net output is gross output minus intermediate
inputs, that is the value of all the goods and services purchased
from outside agriculture and used in the production of its output.
If we measure net output at constant prices then we get a measure
of the contribution of agriculture to the goods and services
produced in the UK. Over our fifteen-year period 1954–68, this
increased at 2.7 per cent per annum, slightly faster, that is, than
gross output. Over the more recent period it has grown more slowly
at about 0.8 per cent per annum 1967–77 and much more slowly
than gross output. The implication of this is that over the last
decade the growth of real output has slowed down markedly but
the growth of agricultural prices has sharply increased. A prime
cause of the rise in prices has been our entry to the EEC, discussed
in the last chapter. Since 1973, gross output has increased by 104
per cent at current prices but has declined by 7 per cent at constant
prices.

Even at the lower recent growth rates, still less at the faster ones
experienced earlier, output has outstripped the rise in consumer
demand. The demand for foodstuffs tends to rise only very slowly.
Home production has been used instead to displace imported
foodstuffs so that the UK has become increasingly self-sufficient in
those foods that it can produce. In 1955 home production
constituted 62 per cent of supplies of indigenous foodstuffs –
those, that is, that we could produce ourselves. By 1968 this had
risen to 64 per cent and by 1975 to 68 per cent. In 1976, due to
exceptional conditions, there was a sharp fall-back.

Although agriculture has grown faster in the post-war period
than between the wars, it has failed to keep pace with the output
of services and manufactured goods where demand has of course
been growing. In consequence the importance of agriculture in the
UK economy, as in all advanced countries, has continued its long-
run decline. In 1950 agriculture accounted for 5.8 per cent of gross
domestic product. By 1968 this had fallen to 3 per cent. Despite the
stagnation of the economy since that date, the decline has
continued. In 1981 the share was down to 2.3 per cent.

To maintain an increase in supply in the face of static demand
the government must do one of two things. Either it must increase

the level of protection offered to agriculture, thus as it were, increasing the competitiveness of British farmers by increasing the disadvantage faced by foreign supplies in the UK market. Or it must raise the real competitiveness of British agriculture by raising productivity. In practice the government has tended to follow both lines together. As discussed in Chapter 4, the level of protection was increased during the 1950s and early 1960s by increasing the levels of guaranteed prices relative to import prices until the budgetary cost became politically embarrassing. Emphasis was then switched towards a system of tariffs and import quotas which raised the price of imported foodstuffs and concealed the cost of support by transferring the burden of support from the taxpayer to the consumer.

The adoption of the CAP was, in a sense, the logical culmination of this policy. The level of protection was raised further by joining the EEC. But the extent to which agricultural protection can be raised by this route also is limited. Higher prices meet consumer resistance. High inflation and expensive food are politically embarrassing and electorally damaging and give rise to wage claims which undermine competitiveness across the board and not merely in agriculture. Successive British governments have shown varying degrees of resistance to rises in Community price levels. The decline in the value of the pound led to a fall in the level of agricultural protection since Community prices on which subsidies are paid are fixed in a common currency unit and are not tied to the value of sterling. The recent response of the British government has been to manipulate the value of the 'green pound', the exchange rate between sterling and the Units of Account of the CAP so as to maintain or improve the value of protection for UK farmers; but this has meant raising food prices to UK consumers, bringing thereby the disadvantages already mentioned. The CAP does not place all of the burden of support on consumers. Surpluses are endemic to the system and their disposal is paid for by budgetary contributions from the member governments. At the time of writing, the British government is attempting to reduce its contribution.

To increase the competitiveness of agriculture via the other route, its efficiency has to be raised not merely relative to that of agriculture in other countries, but productivity must increase at a faster rate than does productivity in the rest of the UK economy. If that does not happen then the competitiveness of agriculture will continue to fall and, to maintain the growth of farmers' incomes even in line with those of other sectors of the Community, the level of protection must be increased.

This is the dilemma that the government has faced. It has had a commitment to raise farmers' incomes, a commitment that it has honoured more than most, and since it has not been able to increase efficiency at a sufficiently rapid rate, it has had to increase protection. As noted, there are limits to the extent to which this can be done. Furthermore, the attempt to do so can damage the competitiveness of other sections of the economy. If protection is via consumer prices then this is directly inflationary and via its effects on wage claims can undermine the competitiveness of manufacturing. If it is done via budgetary subventions then either the tax bill is increased (given the claims of other uses of taxation), which means that individuals' tax rates rise – which again can lead to higher wage claims – or the government borrowing requirement and ultimately the money supply will increase, which again is inflationary.

Apart from these indirect effects there are some direct ones. First, investment funds are being transferred into agriculture when they could be put to more productive use elsewhere. Between 1966 and 1976, gross domestic fixed capital formation in agriculture averaged 17 per cent of the level in manufacturing, while gross domestic product was only 9.5 per cent of the manufacturing level. Not all of this investment would have been available for manufacturing with a lower level of agricultural protection, but some of it would have been.

Perhaps more serious than the misallocation of investment has been the attraction of institutional and other funds into agricultural land purchase in recent years (discussed in more detail in Chapter 8). These funds are a major source of capital for industry. Their attraction into land represents a reduction in the supply available for productive uses in industry. It has been a direct consequence of a high level of support, particularly within the EEC, and the insulation of farming from the effects of economic recession together with tax concessions offered for holding capital in the form of agricultural land. It has resulted in rapidly rising land values which have not always been to the advantage of the farmers themselves.

One final direct effect of the policy of farm income maintenance has been the retention and attraction of entrepreneurial and managerial talent into farming to the detriment particularly of small businesses in what from the nation's viewpoint would be more profitable activities. Productivity is measured as net output per unit of primary input, primary input being the factors of production of economic theory: land, labour and capital. There are severe difficulties in the way of measuring productivity, arising particularly from the problems of measuring capital. In consequence partial measures such as output per unit of labour or output per acre are often used as proxies. In agriculture at least, such partial measures, as we shall see, lead one seriously astray.

Comprehensive measurement of productivity has been undertaken at Cambridge.[1] Over the period 1948–68, at constant prices, agricultural productivity grew at 1.6 per cent per annum. Over the same period productivity in manufacturing grew at 1.8 per cent per annum. While the difference may seem small it implies that at the end of the twenty years, productivity in manufacturing had increased by 49 per cent more than that of agriculture and the competitiveness of the latter had declined accordingly. This is so despite the fact that in international terms the performance of UK manufacturing was unimpressive.

Since 1968 growth of productivity in agriculture has declined to below 1 per cent per annum. The recession makes it difficult to calculate manufacturing productivity growth, but on the crude evidence available there is certainly no reason to think that the relative performance of agriculture has improved. The balance of probability is that it has worsened.

The growth of productivity in agriculture has not been achieved by economizing equally on all inputs to the productive process. It is convenient to group the inputs into four classes: land, labour, capital and chemicals. In these terms productivity growth has been achieved by economizing particularly on land and labour, so that growth of output per acre and per head has been very high, but this has been done by using large quantities of machinery, buildings and chemicals.

The quantity of land devoted to agriculture has fallen throughout the post-war period. About 50,000 acres have gone out of production annually in England and Wales, under a half of the loss being to urban development. Land productivity – output per acre – has risen more rapidly than productivity as a whole. Excluding rough grazings from acreage, it increased at 3 per cent per annum 1958–68 at constant prices. Crop yields have increased at between 2.5 and 3.5 per cent per annum and output of livestock per acre of grass at about 3.5 per cent per annum.

As with land, the quantity of labour used in agriculture has fallen continuously. The agricultural labour force fell by 423,000 between 1950 and 1967, from 5.1 to 3 per cent of the working population. This decline has continued. The rate of increase in labour productivity has been very rapid. The Cambridge study already referred to puts it at 6.4 per cent per annum over the period 1948–68, in comparison with 2.7 per cent for manufacturing industry.

The performance of labour productivity is often cited as the great achievement of post-war agriculture and as a vindication of the policies pursued. It is hard to see why this particular measure should be singled out. As already noted, it does not reflect the performance of productivity as a whole. The other side of the coin from high land and labour productivity has been low capital productivity. This has fallen in all industries according to the Cambridge study but in agriculture it has fallen much faster than elsewhere – at 2 per cent per annum in comparison with 0.6 per cent per annum in manufacturing. Since this calculation includes land with capital and land productivity has risen rapidly, the true rate of decline of capital productivity in agriculture has been at a faster rate than this. Land is not an important input into manufacturing.

Turning to look at farming's use of chemicals, fertilizer usage has risen rapidly – at about 5 per cent per annum. Fertilizer productivity has also therefore been falling – at about 2.5 per cent per annum. Curiously there is little information about the other category of chemical inputs, pesticides,[2] but from what little can be culled from official reports it is clear that their use has been rising much faster than output so that productivity of chemical inputs as a whole is undoubtedly falling.

One argument that is used for the importance of rapidly growing labour productivity is that it permits labour to be released from agriculture for employment in other industries. Two points need to be made here. First, increasing labour productivity is not the only way of releasing labour from agriculture. The alternative is to reduce the rate of growth of output. Labour has been reduced while output expanded, and expanded at a rate which was greater than the expansion in the country's demand for food. Before one can regard this as satisfactory one needs to know whether expanding agricultural output was an efficient use of the nation's resources.

This leads to the second point. While industry has been provided with labour released from agriculture it has at the same time been deprived of capital absorbed in agriculture. If the limit to expansion of industry has been a shortage of labour, which at least in the context of over 3 million unemployed does not seem very plausible, then the policy may have helped economic growth – although the possibility that more labour could have been released by slower growth of agricultural output with rapid growth of labour productivity needs to be considered. On the other hand, if industry has been hampered by a shortage of capital then the policy has hindered economic growth. Economists would normally say that if resources could be used more efficiently in one industry than another then the price mechanism will ensure that resources are transferred. But the flow of resources into and out of agriculture has been largely determined by government through changes in the subsidy system. Without this support the industry would undoubtedly be smaller than it is now. One is left with the conclusion that it has been the government's view that the expansion of agriculture was in the national interest. This is a view that we seriously question.

Government policy has not merely determined the extent of agricultural expansion: it has also determined the form that the expansion has taken. It has worked on the assumption that the best way to raise agricultural productivity is by substituting capital and chemicals for labour and land and the structure of subsidies and farm management advice has been directed to that end. The hope was that increasing capital intensity would leave the industry in a position where it was more competitive and hence needed less protection. As already noted, that has not happened.

Capital intensity of agriculture was encouraged so as to allow the industry to realize economies of scale. Scale economies occur when as a result of expansion it becomes possible to use resources more efficiently. What was being applied to agriculture was a version of what economists call the 'infant industry' argument. Protection of an infant industry is justified if it allows it to gain economies of scale as a result of which productivity would rise, unit costs fall and the industry would be able to compete more effectively with foreign suppliers. An infant industry is usually thought of as a new industry starting on a small scale. Agriculture is not an obvious candidate for an infant industry; rather it is our oldest declining industry. It is extremely doubtful whether there are economies of scale to be realized in agriculture. A survey by Colin Clark[3] suggests that their opposite, decreasing returns, are a universal phenomenon.

There are three possible sources of economies of scale in agriculture. First, expansion of farm size may enable existing equipment to be used more efficiently, e.g. a small farm may be unable to make proper use of a tractor. Second, expansion may permit the use of more specialized equipment; and third, expansion may allow specialization of the workforce: the division of labour effect. Thus a specialized wheat farmer may be more efficient at growing wheat than a farmer who must do many other things besides. But in addition to these sources of scale economies, agriculture is characterized by economies of joint production. Examples are the savings to be realized from crop and crop/meat rotations where one part of a rotation puts back into the soil nutrients that another has taken out or the manure from stock rearing supplies the fertilizer for crops. The exploitation of joint economies has been very important historically in the development of British agriculture: the corn-sheep husbandry of the Downs, Norfolk rotations, etc. Economies of scale are distinct but compatible with joint economies. Increasing farm size under a mixed farming system might give economies of scale without interfering with the economies of joint production.

In fact this policy option was closed by Ministry policy. Increases in farm size have contributed little to the post-war development of agriculture. Some increases have occurred, but in 1976 50 per cent of the farms were still below 50 acres in size. The incentives for farm amalgamation have been weak and have been wholly swamped by other aspects of the subsidy system which have been directed towards maintaining incomes (though in reality mainly pumping up land prices) and encouraging specialization within existing farms. The support system has encouraged specialization by increasing the profitability of some products against others and by the bias in subsidies in favour of capital inputs; specialized equipment and buildings can only be used for one purpose. The extensive system of farm management advice, and the rest of the considerable propaganda service, have been directed towards encouraging specialization. The consequence is that economies of joint production have been sacrificed for dubious economies of specialization. Economies of scale are usually realized when the size of the firm expands. The extent to which they can be realized through specialization without increases in firm size is probably extremely limited in any industry. In agriculture, economies of joint production are probably much more marked than in other industries. Specialization means that they will be lost. The neglect of joint economies in favour of specialization was not felt by the farming industry. The level of protection was adjusted so as to yield them at least reasonable returns under the husbandry they were practising. The costs of increased specialization were borne by the community. Aside from the losses of amenity and ecological damage already described, there were the costs of sewage disposal resulting from the breaking of crop/stock rotations and the intensive rearing of animals and the growing of crops on different farms. In 1967 the flow of sewage in the Severn River catchment area from pigs and cattle was equivalent to that of a city of 300,000 people.[4] This problem fell mainly on ratepayers, among whom farmers were noticeable by their absence. The cost of supplying artificial fertilizer to replace the natural stuff on specialist arable farms, and the pesticides to deal with the expansion of specialist pests on specialist crops, fell via the protection system on the taxpayer and ultimately on the consumer.

Why did the Ministry choose this route for agricultural development? It must be emphasized that the Ministry chose it. Agriculture in the UK has been, and is, a hothouse industry. Without the protection offered it, it would have declined both in output and labour force and land could well, at the margin of cultivation, have gone out of production. MAFF determined its rate of expansion, chose the direction it should take and through a system of subsidies and farm management advice brought it about. Increased specialization entailed increased intensity with the concomitant social and environmental consequences discussed in Chapter 2.

The first point is that an alternative route would have meant a more rapid decline in the number of farmers and as a pressure group the National Farmers' Union, which was naturally opposed to a decline in its membership, probably surpasses any other lobby for effectiveness. Additionally there is a strong sentiment among the public at large in favour of a prosperous agricultural industry, together with a 'gut' belief in the desirability of self-sufficiency in food production, which the NFU was able to exploit.

Second, on an analogy with manufacturing industry, the Ministry probably believed (and still believes) that the only path to increased productivity is via increased specialization and the use of modern specialized equipment resulting in increased capital intensity. This analogy fails to recognize the peculiar features of agriculture: that alone among industries it is an extensive user of land; equally that it is peculiarly subject to the vagaries of the climate which determine within limits what can be produced; that it is subject to complex inter-relationships between products which we have called joint economies; and that it is, and remains, despite the rises in labour productivity, a labour-intensive industry.

The third reason is that the Ministry was also sensitive to the agricultural supply industries: the suppliers of farm machinery and chemicals. The policy was the preferred one from their viewpoint and they have undoubtedly made large profits from it. (There was no profit to them from the exploitation of joint economies: increased use of animal manure and efficient rotation would have meant a lower demand for fertilizers; the effect of these practices in containing diseases would have meant less demand for pesticides and a greater variety of enterprises on the farm would have made farmers more resistant to the charms of specialized plant and machinery.) The profits made by the supply industries come ultimately from the taxpayer. In the course of making these profits they have contributed to UK exports but it is open to question whether the additional exports have not been achieved at too high a cost and could not have been achieved in other commodities had we not had the UK agricultural policy.

The final reason stems from the fact that in order to raise productivity the Ministry sought to bring science to bear in agriculture. New techniques of husbandry have been developed in the agricultural research institutes, on the experimental farms and in the universities. Most of this research has therefore been paid for by the taxpayer. Some of the research has been done in the laboratories and on the farms of the agricultural supply industries since new techniques have usually involved the use of new machinery and equipment or chemicals. Given the support systems, the cost of this too has ultimately fallen on the taxpayer. The dissemination of these techniques lies with the advisory services, both national and commercial ones. Crudely what happens is that the agricultural scientist discovers the technique and the farm management advisory services persuade the farmer to adopt it.

Now, the scientists' criteria of efficiency are physical not economic ones: they are interested in crop yields, conversion coefficients of stock, milk yields and so on. They ask questions of the form: how can I increase the number of cows kept on a given acreage? or the quantity of milk got from a given number of cows? In general terms the answer is obvious: increase the quantities of other inputs. Now, the input of labour is not increased: the scientist is not interested in labour-intensive techniques and in fact increasing the efficiency of labour, i.e. raising output per head, is an aim of the scientist along with increasing the efficiency of land or stock. The impact of science on agriculture is therefore the same as on any other industry: it encourages capital-intensive production. The scientist mainly raises productivity in agriculture by increasing fertilizer, pesticides, concentrated feeds, plant and machinery. Given its role, the direction of development towards increasing use of artificial inputs to save labour and land is scarcely surprising.

In the Community's interest new techniques should only be adopted if they increase *economic* efficiency. This is determined if we know the costs to the Community and not merely to the farmer of the extra resources saved and used. It is determined also if we know the impact of the technique on productivity and not merely on labour productivity or crop yields. But no one asks these questions. The farm management adviser determines whether it is profitable to the farmer but this is evaluated within a set of subsidies – a system of protection – which is designed to encourage just these sorts of techniques. Some inputs – capital, fertilizers – are subsidized but others – labour, rents – are not. Furthermore the specialization of product, which the scientist assumes in order to carry out his or her experiments, is assumed to be desirable. The farm management adviser assumes it and the structure of protection assumes it. No one asks whether specialization is *per se* economic and certainly no one asks whether productivity might not be higher with larger farms. The advice is *to the farmer with a given farm*.

The time has come to sum up the argument of this chapter. In so far as agricultural policy was designed to make agriculture more competitive and hence to reduce its need for protection it has failed. Entry into the EEC entails a recognition of that failure, since EEC agricultural policy is not concerned with competitiveness but with guaranteeing farmers' incomes and ensuring self-sufficiency within an economic blockade. (There was a document, known as the Mansholt Report, that proposed a reconstruction of European agriculture, involving an increase in farm size and the taking out of some thirteen million acres of land from agricultural use. This document gathered dust on a shelf in Brussels before it was forgotten altogether. There is also of course a structural component of the FEOGA budget but it is minute in comparison with the price support expenditure.) The attempt at increasing competitiveness and still more its failure, with concomitant increases in protection, have probably damaged the competitiveness of manufacturing industry. Agriculture, as the NFU never tires of telling us, is Britain's biggest industry. (The NFU is somewhat less forthcoming about the criteria for measuring size that they use to reach that conclusion. On most measures the UK is one of those countries where agriculture is not the largest industry. The policy followed has involved the application of science to production within an existing distribution of farm size. This has involved specialization and intensification of production with the maximization of output per head and output per acre. This policy is the one that has maximized the damage to the environment and to the interests of other users of the countryside. Their interests have been regarded at best as irrelevant and have generally been treated with contempt. That taxpayers have any rights in the countryside and that other uses of farmland have any economic value have not for a moment been considered. This policy of specialization has entailed the neglect of the benefits of mixed farming. A strategy of less intensity and specialization would have reduced the conflict between agriculture and other users of the countryside, reduced the largely hidden costs of agricultural policy, but have implied a lower output, fewer farmers and probably less agricultural wealth.

Notes

1 University of Cambridge, Department of Applied Economics (1974) 'A programme for growth, 12; structural change in the British economy 1948–68'.
2 The MAFF say that this information is confidential to the farmers concerned.
3 Clark, C. (1969) 'The value of agricultural land', *Journal of Agricultural Economics*, vol. XX, no. 1, pp. 1–19.
4 C. T. Riley (1967) 'Farm Waste Disposal', *Agriculture*, vol. 17, no. 1, pp. 59–65.

7

The case for agricultural expansion

We have so far in this book developed a critique of current agricultural policies and have pointed up their undesirable consequences. In this chapter we consider the arguments in support of current policies.

At the outset it is important to distinguish between arguments justifying a high level of protection for agriculture and those justifying the expansion of home agriculture. Amongst the latter it is important also to distinguish arguments for UK self-sufficiency, or for an increase in the degree of self-sufficiency as a primary goal of policy, and those that favour expansion on other grounds.

The two threads of high protection and expansion are of course intertwined. We argued in Chapter 6 that continuous expansion of agricultural production could only be achieved through high and rising levels of protection since, despite a substantial amount of propaganda to the contrary, agricultural productivity had not, and almost certainly would not, increase at the rate of productivity elsewhere in the economy. Furthermore, the nature of postwar agricultural policies has meant that rising agricultural incomes could only be achieved through increases in output since support and subsidy are output related. But there is no logical necessity for this linkage. As we discuss in Chapter 8, it is possible to design policies that maintain or increase agricultural incomes via income maintenance subsidies with constant or declining agricultural output.

Maintenance of agricultural incomes has been the classic justification for support policies. The argument runs as follows. The demand for foodstuffs is income-inelastic, that is to say, with rising incomes people spend smaller proportions of their incomes on food, devoting instead increasing proportions of their expenditure to manufactured goods and services. In conjunction with this fairly static demand for agricultural produce, the competitive nature of the agricultural industry with large numbers of producers each supplying only a tiny proportion of the market means that increases in productivity result in falling prices rather than rising profits for the farmers. The result is that in the absence of support, incomes in the agricultural sector tend to fall relative to those in manufacturing and services. Considerations of equity, therefore, require support for farmers in order to provide a fair distribution of incomes between agriculture and industry, and, since agriculture is the major rural industry, to maintain an equitable distribution between the urban and the rural areas.[1]

Note that this argument does not provide a case for agricultural expansion. Indeed income distribution arguments give no guidance whatsoever about the desirable level of agricultural production. Maintaining UK farmers' share of the home market would require a rate of growth of output approximately equal to that of the rate of population growth; the growth of output actually achieved has been two to three times that level.

As the last section of Chapter 4 demonstrated, if the objective of policy was to maintain a balance between the incomes of farmers and other occupational groups, it has resulted in overkill. Relative to male manual workers, farmers' incomes have increased markedly over the post-war period and they have been maintained when the relative incomes of most non-manual workers and particularly professional workers have been falling. On the other hand if we consider agricultural workers as representing the rural poor, policies have at best prevented a decline relative to manual workers in manufacturing industry. Agricultural workers' earnings in our most recent period (1973–7) have averaged only three-quarters of those of male manual workers. To this rise in farmers' incomes must be added, for the landowner, a hundredfold capital gain and the creation of a capital asset which, almost more than any other, can claim to be inflation proof.

But if one is considering questions of equity it is necessary to consider the incidence of the burden of agricultural support. On this, the study by Josling and Hamway[2] is highly revealing and is worth quoting.

As a proportion of income, the incidence of support costs declines sharply as incomes increased. Two-adult families with no children in the lowest income bracket bear costs equivalent to 5.75% of final income, whilst the same type of household within the high-income range pays only 0.137% of total income in higher consumer prices. The proportion of costs to income also increases slightly with family size.

Agricultural support, particularly under the import levy regime of the CAP is highly regressive.

Whatever the achievements of the policy, the case for supporting farm incomes on grounds of equity is open to question. Why should justice require support for farmers but not – to take another self-employed group who actually *are* declining – small shopkeepers? Industrial policies of governments of all political persuasions have accepted the need for public support to achieve orderly rundown of declining industries. But only in agriculture is it accepted that protection from international competition should be permanent and that the industry instead of declining should grow.

The second argument for support of agriculture is the so-called social one. Support policies are needed to maintain employment in remote rural areas and thereby to prevent rural depopulation. This argument cannot be used to justify support for the agricultural industry as a whole but only those bits of it that are located in remote rural areas. Such specific support exists (for example, the additional grants for 'less favoured areas') but it is offset by grants that have the opposite effect and in any case it constitutes only a tiny proportion of the total volume of agriculture support. Various studies of the CAP have shown that the principal beneficiaries are large farmers; the small farmer, particularly the livestock farmer on marginal land, has benefited least and has not experienced the growth of income of the industry as a whole. As was shown in Chapter 5, the level of effective protection on sheep, a crucial commodity for any strategy against depopulation, has been low in comparison with the principal arable products and other forms of livestock. We now have the further fact that, as the 1981 Census[3] showed, the process of urban decentralization is producing population growth in all but two of the rural districts of England and Wales including the most remote ones.

One final comment on this argument. The trends initiated by current policies towards arable farming, particularly cereals, and away from small-scale livestock enterprises, is employment destroying rather than creating. The usual measures of the employment effects of agriculture are the Standard Man Days (SMDs) per annum of work generated by various agricultural enterprises. For cereals the labour requirement per hectare is 2.5 SMDs if straw is gathered and 1.75 SMDs if it is burnt or ploughed in.[4] A dairy herd with followers at an average stocking rate of 1.75 cows per hectare would require approximately 14 SMDs per hectare, and sheep rearing approximately 6 SMDs per hectare.

Thus the case for agricultural protection, and particularly for the monstrously high levels that at present exist, is to say the least shaky. One must look for its justification to the case for expansion of agricultural output, and to this we now turn. Arguments here may be classed into three groups: the (short-term) balance of payments case; longer-term strategic considerations which mainly revolve around increasing the degree of self-sufficiency in food production; and the argument from altruism. The line of argument which says that we should expand home agriculture in order to redress the balance between disbursements and receipts within the EEC budget could perhaps be treated as a fourth. It is separate from, but closely allied to, the balance of payments argument.

Balance of payments problems from their nature are temporary affairs, although they may be chronic in the sense that they persistently recur, e.g. whenever the economy expands. Many commentators believe or did, at least until the advent of North Sea oil, that this is so with the UK economy; but none, so far as we are aware, has seriously argued for agricultural expansion as a means of reducing the economy's propensity to experience balance of payments problems, as opposed to dealing with whatever crisis we were currently experiencing. But if such an argument does not exist, it may easily be invented. We deal with it below when we consider the strategic arguments of which it is a possible version.

Even if the UK's balance of payments problems are not chronic, agricultural expansion as a means of coping with a balance of payments crisis is. Arguments for it recur every time the elimination of a balance of payments deficit becomes a policy priority.

Since the UK is a net importer of foodstuffs, an expansion of home agriculture may be expected to reduce imports or increase exports or both, since we simultaneously import and export agricultural produce; in any case it may be expected to reduce our net imports of foodstuffs. The improvement in the balance of payments afforded by agricultural expansion is considerably less than the direct reduction in net imports, however, since some agricultural inputs, such as fertilizers, pesticides or animal feeds, have a high import content; and in addition some of the commodities consumed in agriculture, e.g. fuel oils, would otherwise be exported. None the less most studies suggest that even allowing for the induced imports, agricultural expansion is in general import-saving in the short run, i.e. it is a possible means of improving the balance of payments over a time horizon of 1–3 years. But there is an opportunity cost to agricultural expansion; the resources absorbed in agriculture could instead have been used in some other activity to save imports or increase exports and it is far from clear that expanding agriculture is the most efficient way to improve the balance of payments.

There are really three issues here. First, agricultural expansion draws resources from other activities and therefore has an indirect effect on net exports in other industries: had the resources remained where they were, they would have contributed to exports or saved imports of other commodities. A number of studies have taken account of this effect and have concluded that even allowing for it, agricultural expansion still improves the balance of payments.

Second, instead of taking these resources and putting them into agriculture, we could have taken them and put them into some other activity. Had we done so, could we have achieved an even greater balance of payments turnround or the same turnround in the same time? The answer to this question depends on the particular period one is considering, the range of options under consideration and the institutional and legal constraints on the options. On all this the various studies of agriculture's import-saving role are silent. Some general points may be made, however, which suggest that agriculture is probably not the best place to put your funds if you want to improve the balance of payments. First, the production period in agriculture, the time between the commitment of resources and the appearance of the extra output is long relative to the average of manufacturing activities. Second, output is uncertain in agriculture being subject *inter alia* to the vagaries of the weather. Third, comparative advantage lies with industry and certain key exporting services, not agriculture, and it is probably a good rule, in the absence of more precise information, to devote your resources to the activities in which you are most, rather than least, competitive.

This last point leads to our third consideration. Committing resources to short-run balance of payments improvement has a long-run opportunity cost. Agricultural expansion requires considerable commitment of capital which is then not available elsewhere. We have already described in Chapter 6 how agricultural expansion could be seen as an attempt at altering comparative advantage in its favour, bringing about the expansion of an industry that under international competition would have declined. The cost of this is a reduction in the competitiveness of UK manufacturing. The extent to which agricultural policy is to blame for the poor performance of UK manufacturing is yet to be determined. That it has to take some of the blame seems to us to be clear. The long-term cost is to be seen of course not merely in industry but, as we have seen, in substantial and, for the most part, irreversible damage to the environment.

The classic case for devoting resources to import saving is when for some reason it is not possible to alter the exchange rate to bring payments into balance. The rationale for import saving now that we have a freely floating exchange rate is then unclear in any case. It makes some sense with fixed exchange rates if there are significant costs, psychological or otherwise, to altering the exchange rate. Agricultural expansion cannot be an alternative to import controls as a means of reducing the balance of payments constraint on the reduction of unemployment;[5] in terms of resource use it operates against such a policy rather than with it.

Given that import saving via agricultural expansion would be justified if the currency is overvalued, one may calculate the extent to which the currency would have to be overvalued if a specific expansion programme were to be justified. One of us made such a calculation for a proposed reclamation of part of The Wash at Gedney Drove End in Lincolnshire.[6] To justify that particular scheme the £ would have had to be 30 per cent overvalued; a state of affairs which, if ever observed, could not persist with a floating exchange rate.

The final point to be made on the balance of payments case concerns the question of the UK contribution to the EEC budget. The UK is subject to the CAP regime and, so it is argued, an expansion of UK agriculture will lead to a transfer of funds from the Community to the UK in the form of additional agricultural subsidy. The value to the UK of an increase in output is not the world price of the product, as would normally be the case, but the subsidized EEC price, since the difference, the subsidy to the farmer, is derived from the central budget and is thus a transfer to the UK from the rest of the Community. That is the argument; it appears to be believed by MAFF, at least on the evidence of their instructions to water authorities in their cost-benefit appraisals of proposed drainage schemes to value the extra agricultural output at the prices received by farmers.[7] It is probably underlying the thinking in the White Papers of 1975 and 1979, *Food from Our Own Resources* (Cmnd 6020) and *Farming and the Nation* (Cmnd 7458). Some doubts about its validity might creep in when one realizes that one might easily substitute France or Germany for the UK in the argument, and indeed it might be applied simultaneously by all countries together.

All the major products of UK agriculture are in surplus within the EEC. An increase in UK production will not cause UK or EEC consumers to eat more; it will either displace third country (i.e. non-EEC) imports or, in one way or another, add to EEC surpluses.[8] In the former case the EEC budgetary authorities lose revenue equal to the levies on previous imports without a concomitant reduction in expenditure. In the latter they incur additional expenditure for storage and disposal plus the export subsidy without a concomitant increase in revenue. Given that the authorities are operating a budget this imbalance must be redressed. What are the sources of their funds? There are three basic sources: the agricultural levies, customs duties on third country non-agricultural imports, and the proceeds of a 1 per cent VAT. Some additional revenue will accrue to the authorities automatically from the additional VAT and customs revenue duties paid out of the incomes generated in the UK from agricultural expansion, but these cannot be sufficient to redress the balance. The authorities will thus be forced either to cut down on non-agricultural spending, part of which will come from the UK, or to raise extra revenue. Either way part of the extra subsidies received by UK farmers as a result of agricultural expansion fall on UK consumers. A first guess might be that it would be equal to the UK's share of total EEC consumer spending on non-food items but this would be an underestimate for two reasons: because of the automatic element already referred to and because the UK has a higher propensity to import from third countries than the rest of the EEC. Some trial calculations suggest that between 26 and 46 per cent of the extra subsidies received by UK farmers from agricultural expansion will be paid for by UK consumers.[9] Thus, far from being a free good, agricultural expansion adds considerably to the burden of agricultural support met by UK consumers.

If governments choose to ignore this extra burden, they can still improve the balance between receipts and expenditure on the EEC budget by expanding agriculture. In fact, since no single EEC country contributes half of the revenue, all can individually improve their balances by such expansion. The result is burgeoning surpluses and increasingly heavy burdens on EEC consumers, and a broadly regressive transfer of income from the urban poor to the agrarian rich. This is the basic flaw in the Common Agricultural Policy.

We have now dealt with the first and fourth arguments in favour of expansion. We now turn to the second, the strategic case.

The strategic argument for self-sufficiency in agricultural produce has a long pedigree (as the quotations from the controversy on the Corn Laws in the next chapter demonstrate) and has taken many forms. In the early post-war years it was seen as a protection against future wars and particularly the sort of submarine blockade that was the subject of the Battle of the Atlantic. Whether even in 1942 it was lost imports of food as opposed to strategic materials and armaments that was the major threat to the war effort is questionable, but in any case it seems likely that changes in military technology have rendered the argument obsolete. Furthermore, the method by which output has been increased has rendered agriculture itself highly dependent on imports and hence vulnerable to blockade. At times of dock strikes and fuel crises the agricultural industry has been seen to be amongst the first to cry for relief. Thus the assumption that increases in UK food production mean increases in self-sufficiency in the sense of independence of international trade is patently false. Increased self-sufficiency could be achieved without increases in output by moving to a technology that made production less dependent on chemical inputs and manufactured animal feeds.

Before commenting on current versions of the strategic argument two general points need making:

(i) We have not been, and, at currently acceptable levels of nutrition, cannot be self-sufficient in the major foodstuffs at current population levels. We are currently self-sufficient in liquid milk, eggs and poultry and, virtually so, in feed grains.

(ii) In joining the EEC we have entered a system of self-sufficient high-cost producers, but have left a system of self-sufficient low-cost producers (the 'old' Commonwealth). We are at present eliminating our 'dependency' on New Zealand, Australia and Canada. That was a system properly of mutual interdependence. In the EEC we could be said to have truly entered a system of dependence.

The current version of the strategic argument is that we need agricultural expansion in order to protect ourselves against a coming world shortage of foodstuffs as populations increase and industrialization leads to a drying up of present world supplies.

If a world food crisis is coming, for the west at least it is not here now. While there are periodic failures of the grain harvest and sporadic policy-induced shortages in such things as beef and potatoes, the general situation in temperate foodstuffs is that of surplus, with, for the Common Market, the notorious mountains and lakes – not, unfortunately, a landscape of much value for recreation – and such wonders as the feeding of butter to cows, or denaturing of sugar with garlic to sell cheaply to beekeepers.

Agricultural expansion in Britain and the EEC is forcing industrialization on the efficient suppliers of temperate foodstuffs, inducing thereby the very crisis it is allegedly insuring against. Even if we accept that a hypothetical future crisis must be guarded against, present agricultural policies are not the way to do it. The extra output is not required now. The important thing, presumably, is to keep the land in 'good heart' and to safeguard the elasticity of British supply. A reduction of current output and, certainly, a return to less intensive techniques of mixed farming seems more likely to do this.

Part of the appeal of the strategic argument rests on the assumption that, in the absence of a policy of agricultural expansion, the agricultural land will disappear under bricks and mortar. This is manifest nonsense. (An interesting sidelight on this is the work of Robin H. Best (1981) writing in *Land Use and Living Space*,[10] where it is shown that gardens produce as much food per unit area as British agriculture anyway.) The land used for housing, roads and other non-industrial uses is not affected one way or another by agricultural policy, although it is by planning policies, and any extra requirements of industry resulting from a release of resources from agriculture would be small. A reduction in agricultural output would appear as a reduction in the intensity of use of existing agricultural land, just as the agricultural expansion has been brought about by increasing intensity. The only obvious change of land use would be a possible transfer of land from agriculture to forestry. This is taking place in any case in the uplands at an alarming rate – alarming that is for those concerned with the scarce ecosystems that are destroyed thereby – but it is probably best viewed as a shift from fast-yielding to slow-yielding crops with the option for converting back retained. With current European surpluses, a case for converting some of the lowland arable to timber might be made.

According to the study by Best,[11] the percentage of the land area of England and Wales devoted to agriculture fell by 2 per cent from 80.6 per cent to 78.6 per cent between 1950 and 1965. Of this loss over half (1.1 per cent) was attributed to forestry. The other 0.9 per cent was attributed to urban land use, although urban land use increased by 0.9 per cent as a result of a drop from 3.3 to 2.4 per cent in the land 'unaccounted for'. This loss in agricultural land has been trivial when viewed against the increase in output per acre and has not imposed any measurable constraint on the rate of growth of agricultural output. By the year 2000 Edwards and Wibberley[12] forecast a loss of agricultural land equal to 6.2 per cent of the land use for the United Kingdom as a whole. Of this again over half, 3.4 per cent, goes to forestry, and the rest, 2.8 per cent (plus 0.1 per cent from land unaccounted for), to urban uses.

The rates of net transfers of agricultural land to urban use over the period 1960–75 amount, according to Best[13], to 18.3 thousand hectares per annum, and the rate of conversion over the post-war period as a whole amounted to a mere 16,000 hectares per annum. This author found no evidence that the rate of transfer was increasing, although it fluctuated more or less in phase with the trade cycle. Furthermore, much of the transfer of land to urban use does not entail its disappearance under bricks and mortar. Urban use includes, for example, golf courses, airfields, gardens, orchards, and the proportion of new urban land use that is of this form is increasing; much of this is re-convertible to agriculture if the need arises and, as has previously been noted, gardens and allotments are potentially productive of food in any case.

The final argument for agricultural expansion is the altruistic one. It may be simply put. There is starvation in many of the underdeveloped nations of the world. A responsible government has a moral obligation to do what it can to help. Part of this must surely involve maximizing its food output.

Unfortunately this argument ignores the harsh realities of the economic conditions of world agriculture and of world trade. First, as was explained in Chapter 5, agricultural protection in the rich industrial countries severely damages the international markets in foodstuffs by making the swings from glut to shortage far more extreme and price fluctuations much greater. 'Food aid' is too frequently a cynical device for off-loading embarrassing surpluses and the effect is greatly to impair the development of an effective modern agriculture in the developing countries in receipt of the aid. The 'food aid' is geared not to relieving starvation at points of crisis but to bolstering the incomes of the already very rich. It is arguable that more real good would be done by opening the markets of the rich nations to food exports from the Third World and thereby encouraging their development of efficient agricultural systems.

The second problem is that while there may be a need of foodstuffs in the poorest countries of the world, because they are poor, there is no effective demand for them. Where the intention is really to relieve want the food must go as aid. It is far from clear that UK agricultural expansion increases world capacity to provide foodstuffs as aid. As already noted, agricultural expansion in the UK and the EEC leads to a contraction in output in the efficient producers, our previous suppliers. The efficient producers cannot redirect their food as aid since they, like everyone else, can provide aid only from an economic surplus and, lacking the revenue to purchase manufactured products, must direct their resources out of agricultural production for export into industrial expansion. The supply of foodstuffs for aid is maximized by encouraging the expansion by trade of output of the efficient producers; by encouraging the international division of labour.

There is a further aspect to this question. Aid is really necessary to meet crises engendered by wars, floods, droughts, etc., and when the countries affected either lack the funds to obtain the food on world markets or are unable to obtain the required quantity from the market at any price. In a properly functioning international market an exceptional demand simply raises the price of the commodity so that the requirement is met by other buyers either reducing their demands or paying more for them. The protection system operated within the EEC, particularly since the UK has joined it, has greatly damaged the world market for many commodities. The consequence is that a developing country wishing to make an exceptional purchase, e.g. because of a poor monsoon, has no choice but to obtain food aid if surpluses are available. The agricultural protection system creates the demand for the food aid which it then virtuously supplies.

By way of summary we may note that there is one final argument for a policy of agricultural expansion. It improves the incomes of rich farmers and those of the richest farmers most; it generates large capital gains for all rural landowners and increases the turnover and profits of the agricultural supply industries. We are not persuaded, however, that these considerations are sufficient reason for the policy.

Notes

1 There are also arguments that agricultural incomes are highly uncertain because of unpredictable effects of weather and disease on production and because of the violent price fluctuations that occur in uncontrolled commodity markets. These arguments constitute a case for schemes for stabilization of agricultural incomes or agricultural prices but not *per se* for stabilizing them at any level above the average that would hold in an uncontrolled market, i.e. they are not in themselves arguments for *protection*.

2 Josling, T. E. and Hamway, D. (1976) 'Income transfer effects of the Common Agricultural Policy', in Davey, B., Josling, T. E. and McFarquhar, A. (eds) *Agriculture and the State*, London, Macmillan, p. 184.

3 *1981 Census of Population: Preliminary Report, England and Wales* (1982), London, HMSO.

4 These data are taken from Nix, J., (1981) *Farm Management Pocketbook*, 11th edn, Ashford, Kent, Wye College, University of London.

5 See University of Cambridge, Department of Applied Economics (1977 and 1979) *Economic Policy Review*.

6 Evidence by J. K. Bowers to a Public Inquiry into a proposed reclamation at Gedney Drove End, Department of Environment, Inspector's Report, March 1981.

7 This advice would be incorrect even if all the subsidy were a transfer from other EEC countries. The extra agricultural output should still be valued at resource cost (i.e. world market prices) but allowance made for the fact that an income transfer from the rest of the EEC to UK farmers takes place.

8 It might replace other EEC production in which case the additional surplus appears outside the UK, or it might go straight into store as an increment to UK surplus.

9 See Bowers, J. K. (1982) 'Who pays the cost of UK agricultural expansion?', University of Leeds, School of Economic Studies, Discussion Paper no. 110.

10 Best, R. H. (1981) *Land Use and Living Space*, London, Methuen.

11 Best, R. H. (1965) 'Recent changes and future prospects of land use in England and Wales', *Geographical Journal*, 13, pt 1, March; and Best, R. H. (1981), op. cit.

12 Edwards, A. M. and Wibberley, G. P. (1971) *An Agricultural Land Budget for Britain, 1965–2000*, Ashford, Kent, Wye College, University of London.

13 Best, R. H. (1978) 'Myth and reality in the growth of urban land', in Rogers, A. W. (ed.) *Urban Growth, Farmland Losses and Planning*, London, Institute of British Geographers.

8

Options for policy

We have seen that the expansion of UK agriculture in the post war period via increased intensity of exploitation and specialization has resulted in serious damage to the environment and increasing conflict between farmers and other users of the countryside. The theme of this book is that neither the pace nor the direction of agricultural change has been determined by the pressure of market forces. Rather, agriculture is an industry maintained in hothouse conditions and fuelled by public money. Before the UK's entry to the EEC, the direction and pace of change were maintained by the manipulation of price levels and relative prices at the Annual Review and by the use of direct subsidies to encourage intensification and changes of technique. Entry to the EEC introduced an additional location of decision-making and changed the system of protection but did not affect the essential problem. Expansion has been maintained, as throughout the whole post-war period, by fixing prices received by farmers at artificially high levels, though now it is consumers who pay the artificially high prices whereas before the bill was largely met by taxpayers. At the time of UK entry, the level of protection within the EEC tended to be higher than in the UK. More seriously for the environment, the price structure within the EEC has particularly favoured cereals at the expense of livestock and continued to favour capital-intensive methods. The overall level of subsidy has increased the pressure for intensity of land use and intensive methods. But it is probably the case that the importance of direct subsidies on inputs has declined, though those that remain, especially the subsidies for the extension of land drainage and upland 'improvement', have been particularly damaging in that they have been aimed directly at the environmentally least damaged areas. Thus entry into the EEC has, on balance, made the conflict between agriculture and the environment worse, has concealed the costs of support and given several more twists to the through-the-looking-glass logic of agricultural support.

The beneficiaries of this policy have been the farmers and especially landowners – particularly large farmers and arable farmers – and the management and shareholders of the agricultural supply industries. Increasingly also institutions and companies have emerged as landlords to reap the benefit of higher land values,[1] thereby diverting valuable capital into useless land holding. They have benefited at the public expense, since the reason for high land values has been the high level of agricultural support. As we remarked in Chapter 5, policy has quite literally made millionaires from the public purse.

Public awareness of the lunacy of our current level of agricultural support and the growing conflict between agriculture and the countryside has increased since Britain entered the EEC. This is for several reasons, including the spectacle of European butter mountains, enhanced concern for the environment and the fact that the UK entered the EEC as a major food importer and so inevitably pays a substantial share of the cost of European farmers' support. This was to be expected: its value as a vent for embarrassing and costly agricultural surpluses was for the original six members, a major benefit of UK entry. This burden takes the form of a higher cost on the balance of payments, as a result of higher priced food imports, plus an adverse budgetary balance with the EEC because the sum of VAT receipts and tariff revenues transferred to Brussels exceeds the value of export subsidies and other direct payments to UK farmers. Ironically it is this budgetary balance rather than the enormous and unwarranted burden of high support prices on the UK consumer that is the focus of government concern. The row about the over-riding of the UK veto on the 1982 farm price settlement concerned the budgetary balance. No basic objection was raised by the UK to the principle of raising prices by 11 per cent – a rate higher than either forecast rates of inflation or the 4 per cent target for pay increases – in the face of rising surpluses. The Agriculture Minister appeared to have no brief for the UK consumer, only the farmer, despite his being Minister for Fisheries and Food as well. In this our stance was in line with the agricultural ministeries of all other EEC governments, as well as being true to MAFF's traditions as a ministry of farmers, with many ministers themselves being farmers.

But there are perhaps some grounds for hope that the 1982 price settlement may have been the last of its kind; that some curbs will be placed on the avarice and irresponsibility of the farming lobby. The sort of settlement we saw in 1982 was tenable when the economies of western Europe were experiencing rapid or relatively rapid economic growth; they could then afford the high levels of agricultural protection. This is not to say that these levels of protection were or are in any sense justified: they are not, and, as we have shown, the arguments for them are a mosaic of *non sequitur* and distortion; nor that they did not carry the high environmental costs we have discussed; nor again that they were not in conflict with the pursuit of the high economic growth needed to finance them. But the burden of agricultural support upon workers experiencing full employment and growing real incomes was tolerable.

The situation in 1982 was very different; economic growth had virtually stopped, manufacturing output was falling, in the UK rapidly so, and well over 10 per cent of the workforce was unemployed. There was no longer the industrial strength to carry the burden of protection and the costs of farm support increasingly fell on an unemployed urban population. In these circumstances the interests of the conservationists and the consumer are the same. EEC price levels are increasingly regarded as socially unacceptable even by those who are indifferent to their impact on the quality of the environment. The traditional defensive attitudes of conservationists are not and never were tenable. In the final chapter of *Conservation and Agriculture*,[2] Joan Davidson writes:

The idea of conserving those natural resources which have indirect economic value may seem inappropriate in periods of economic stress. The conservation of wildlife and landscape has always been most active at prosperous times in prosperous places and among prosperous people. For Britain in the later seventies it is not an auspicious time to be questioning the expansion of major economic activity like agriculture: there is a continuing uncertainty about the costs and supply of food products from abroad and pressure to intensify the output at home. Farmers face rising input costs for materials, energy and wages, as well as new taxes. In circumstances such as these, suggestions for the modification of some established farming practices which do little or nothing to improve agricultural productivity even though they may limit the further loss of amenity values from the countryside, must seem to some frivolous and impracticable.

The whole tone of this argument is far too apologetic. Furthermore, because it fails to diagnose the basic economic cause of agricultural destruction of the countryside – subsidy-induced prosperity – it wholly misconstrues the problems. There is a hard-nosed economic argument in favour of conservation. Conservation policies, the most effective of which would be a radical restructuring of farm support policies, would achieve a more efficient use of scarce resources. The beauty and natural fecundity of the countryside is a real resource, so too is the recreational use of it. This resource is intangible only in that it seldom commands a market price and so fails to ring up in landowners' cash registers. As any introduction to economics will explain, this constitutes a basic failure of market mechanisms to create an efficient use of resources. In the case of agriculture this problem has been made worse by policy rather than been reduced by it. We have chosen to subsidize precisely those activities – the use of artificial fertilizers, hedgerow removal, land drainage, etc. – which cause the damage to a real resource; and these damage-causing activities are already financially rewarded by the market since they increase saleable output: food. But since we also have subsidized food production, by farm support policies, farmers have been subsidized twice over to despoil the rural environment in the ways documented in Chapters 2 and 3. Common sense and hard-nosed economics suggest a completely contrary policy.

Thus there is no single sentiment in the quotation from Davidson with which we agree. It is not inappropriate to conserve 'those natural resources which have no direct economic value' in times of economic stress or at any other time since the natural resources in question emphatically have economic value. The problem arises because they have no commercial value to those who control them. Down river supplies of fresh water may have no direct economic value to the farmer whose fertilizers pollute the supply, but they are certainly an economic resource. This problem has long been recognized by economists as a basic defect in the market economy and a sound reason at any time for interventionist policies aimed at putting the failure right.

The view that conservation of wildlife and landscape has been most active at times of prosperity is no less misleading. It is prosperity and its concomitant pressure on natural resources which to a large extent create the need for conservation, as John Clare witnessed during the last great phase of agricultural riches in the late eighteenth and early nineteenth centuries. Traditional agricultural methods as developed in Britain and Europe over a period of centuries were more or less in balance with the environment for most of the time. The less prosperous farming was, the less intensive and the less intervention it produced in the natural environment. Dog and stick farming may be hell for farmers and wreak havoc on food production, but it is certainly good for the natural fauna and flora. Prosperity may generate the ability and the desire to direct resources to national parks and nature reserves – activist conservation and amenity policies – but, especially in the context of prosperous and intensive agriculture, it generates the need for such intervention and raises its apparent cost.

But the advocacy of conservation from a prostrate position is already rejected by conservationists, or at least by the professional ones in the RSPB, the CPRE, the County Naturalists Trusts and the Nature Conservancy Council. Their instinct and training argues for a more aggressive stance; the victories over Amberley Wild Brooks and Gedney Drove End reinforced this and the experience of rigorous political lobbying over the Wildlife and Countryside Act has completed the process. The prostrate approach to conservation remains now only in the debates of the merits of persuasion within the existing legislative framework as attempted by the Farming and Wildlife Advisory Group (FWAG) – predicated on the belief that conservation is a matter of no more than information and good-will – and of bribery within the existing framework: the vexed question of compensation. We have nothing to say against the worthy objectives of FWAG, though we observe that in a political climate hostile to conservation its achievements will necessarily be limited. We believe, however, that an effective conservation policy requires above all substantial changes in agricultural policy and it is to these that we now turn. Since the changes we propose would unquestionably reduce both consumer prices and public spending, we see them having a very strong appeal if they are subject to rational analysis rather than pressure group politics.

The single most important change in agricultural policy from the viewpoint of conservation, and the starting point for the formulation of a more rational and socially acceptable agricultural policy, would be a reduction in the level of agricultural protection. This would entail, and indeed within the EEC would be achieved by, a fall in agricultural prices and hence incomes, relative to those of industry. Decreased prosperity in agriculture would lead to decreased land prices and consequently to decreased intensity of exploitation of land and lower capital investment in agriculture. It is this intensity of exploitation, necessitated by high land values, which above all damages the environment and brings agriculture in conflict with other uses of the countryside.

A superficial reading of standard agricultural economics textbooks might lead one to suppose that a fall in farm-gate prices, like a rise in them, would lead to increased intensity of exploitation of the land rather than the reverse. This is the so-called problem of perverse supply response: in the face of falling prices farmers attempt to maintain their incomes by increasing output. If perverse supply exists at all it is at most a short-term (one or two years) problem. Increasing intensity or even maintaining existing levels requires investment and the finance for this comes either out of direct public support or the profits of farming or is attracted into farming from elsewhere in the economy because of the high profits to be earned there. Declining grants, prices and profits would lead to declining investment and ultimately to decreases in output per acre, i.e. to reductions in the intensity of exploitation of the land. The intensive margin in UK agriculture, as well as the extensive one, increases in times of prosperity and retreats in times of depression.

A reduction in the level of protection of UK (and European) agriculture is not a policy of itself, only a necessary component of a more rational policy. Since much of the environmental damage results from the expansion of arable at the expense of pasture – this has been particularly so with the recent decline in the wetlands – conservation requires consideration of the structure of farm prices as well as their level. In the EEC a uniform across-the-board percentage increase in agricultural prices results in a rise in the profitability of arable and especially cereal enterprises relative to livestock enterprises. This is because arable products, particularly grains, are a substantial input into livestock production as an animal feed. Consequently part, and in some cases a major part, of the increase in price of output for the livestock producer is matched by an increase in costs of production. For the arable producer the increase in costs induced by the agricultural price settlement is much smaller, affecting no more than seed costs.

This built-in tendency for cereals to increase in profitability relative to livestock with the typical, uniform, EEC price settlement, is part of the explanation for the extension of the cereal area in recent years. We have already all but lost the chalkland downs and are now seeing serious damage to wetland habitats. The pressures for switching to arable would of course be greater in the face of uniformly falling prices than with rising prices, since the gains to the farmer from switching to more profitable enterprises assume an enhanced significance in these circumstances. Conservation would benefit by a positive discrimination in price fixing in favour of livestock and against cereals.

Cereals for animal feed, and all increases in cereal production are for animal feed since the demand for cereals for human consumption is more or less static, are among the most profitable crops for the farmer. The EEC has a growing surplus in feed grains and even the UK is more than self-sufficient in those that can be grown. A switch from grass to cereal growing – the basis of the alleged benefits from reclaiming, *inter alia*, the marshes of the Norfolk Broads – adds to this surplus supply at the same time as reducing the demand. The absurdity is manifest. Independently of the case for reducing agricultural prices as a whole, a case exists for a substantial reduction in cereal prices to redress the structural imbalance that exists within the CAP.

It is worth noting that the problem of the bias towards increasing profitability of cereal enterprises that exists under the CAP regime did not exist under the pre-CAP guaranteed price system since, in that system, an increase in the price of cereals to the arable farmer did not directly lead to an increase in the cost of cereal products to the livestock producer: the livestock producer could continue to buy at world market prices. Some indirect effects could be traced but their overall impact was unlikely to be significant. We have already noted in Chapter 4 that under the guaranteed price system MAFF was able, by manipulation of price relatives, to alter the structure of production quite rapidly. The CAP system is far less efficient in this regard both because of the political difficulty of manipulating price relatives and because of the impossibility of affecting output prices independently of input costs.

As well as the level and structure of price support, the development of intensive agriculture is encouraged by direct subsidies on inputs into the production process. These subsidies are of two forms: directly to the farmer under the Agriculture and Horticulture Grants Scheme (AHGS) and its various predecessors going back to the Production Grants originally introduced in 1951, and through the mediation of other bodies, particularly by the grants paid to water authorities and internal drainage boards for land drainage. UK entry into the EEC led to a reduction in the importance of direct grants to farmers in the total support package, and some of the most obviously undesirable subsidies, e.g. on fertilizer usage, for hedgerow removal and upland ploughing, have been either removed altogether or are available in more restrictive circumstances. However, field drainage, fencing of open moorland and the euphemistically entitled 'grassland re-generation' continue at an enhanced rate of subsidy in the 'less favoured areas' (previously the Hill Areas). There has, moreover, been substantial growth, under MAFF direction and tutelage, of the destructive activities of the drainage bodies. It is doubtful if a case exists for any further extension of agricultural drainage and probably a good case exists for a retreat in the form of a failure to renew some of the existing drainage works as they wear out. Many are designed to a standard which is greater than necessary to achieve their agricultural objectives and no economic case exists for almost any of the schemes at present proposed and in progress.

Spurious cases are made by various devices which breach the principles of cost-benefit analysis, particularly by measuring benefits at subsidized prices, working with unrealistic theoretical yields, and assuming excessive rates of 'take-up'. The activities of water authorities would be sharply curtailed by the cessation of grant-aid for agricultural drainage; given their powers to get the funds from the public by raising water rates, an instruction from MAFF that agricultural drainage works should cease may perhaps be necessary to supplement this.

The Internal Drainage Boards (IDBs) are a different problem. They are dedicated to using public funds for the benefit of farmers and showing scant sense of responsibility for the interests of conservation or indeed for the interests of the majority of their ratepayers.[3] They have undoubtedly outlived their usefulness and should be abolished. Such of their functions as need to be carried out should be given either to the water authorities, who in any case perform these functions in areas where there are no IDBs or, better, to democratically accountable local authorities. Needless to say, these necessary functions do not include promoting ambitious and uneconomic agricultural drainage schemes.

It is sometimes argued that general capital subsidies to farmers are necessary to maintain equity between agriculture and manufacturing, where capital subsidies exist in the form of tax allowances for investment expenditure. This argument is a nonsense. A misallocation of resources towards agriculture is an inevitable consequence of the price support system: indeed it is an *objective* of the system. Furthermore, grants under AHGS are in addition to the normal tax allowance for investment in industry and agriculture and investment in agriculture is further encouraged by favourable treatment of capital taxation.

The alternative justification for AHGS is that farmers have limited access to investment funds. With current profitability of farming and the increasing participation of industrial companies in investment in land this is, to say the least, dubious. The abolition of agricultural capital grants might make only a minor contribution to a reduction in the growth of agricultural intensity. None the less, it would be a desirable change. And its impact would be greatest in the most marginal areas which tend also to be the wildest and most beautiful and are now under threat of 'improvement'.

The proposals so far have concentrated on a substantial scaling down of the enormous burden of direct and indirect support for agriculture. This is necessary for any programme of reform and would make a major contribution to the protection of the countryside and the natural environment. A radical programme of reform would aim to change the basis of support. The starting point for this is the recognition of the fact that conservation and amenity are joint products with foodstuffs but, because amenity is unpriced, it is under-provided. The problem then is one of what economists would call market failure arising because the environment and the landscape are public goods, by which is meant that it is impossible or impractical to charge consumers of them for their use and that providing a good environment for one 'consumer' does not reduce the quantity available to others. This is not an altogether accurate portrayal of the problem since, as we have seen, it is not that farmers have destroyed the environment and landscape because it yielded them no income. They have been subjected to a barrage of propaganda and advice, coupled with large financial incentives to destroy it. Any farmer resisting these strictures would have tended to be classified as inefficient and backward. Any policy of reform can only work if the arguments for 'scientific' farming are recognized for what they are – naive and frequently spurious, and the powerful pressures for intensification are eliminated. Because this has not been done, the policy embodied in the Wildlife and Countryside Act, 1981 must inevitably fail.

If the problem is that of market failure as described above then the solution is either to tax the farmer for providing agricultural output by environmentally damaging techniques or to subsidize forms of production which conserve the environment. If this is done then the community welfare will be improved since society will get a better, i.e. preferred, mix of agricultural output and amenity. If taxation or subsidy is not feasible then a second-best solution is given by imposing physical, i.e. planning, controls on production techniques and cropping patterns.

The extension of planning controls to agriculture is the solution favoured by Marion Shoard.[4] For areas of high environmental or landscape value she suggests that changes in agricultural practices, e.g. grubbing out hedgerows, draining ponds or ploughing pasture, should require planning consent. Similar suggestions, for

National Parks and SSSIs, were made during the debates on the Wildlife and Countryside Act. The persuasive argument for this approach lies in the analogy between valuable, historic, landscape and environment and listed buildings, where planning consent is required for demolition or damaging alteration. The less than happy experience with the protection of buildings of historical and architectural value should make one view this approach with scepticism. Of itself planning control is a second-best solution. It is never 100 per cent efficient (nor anything close to that level), and controls are costly[5] and difficult to police. If market forces make it profitable to pull down a listed building and neither they nor the planning system provide an incentive for its upkeep then it, at best, falls down from neglect. Economic incentives, if properly designed, are to a greater or lesser degree self-policing and, in the sort of context with which we are dealing, are in general superior to physical controls in influencing human behaviour. A degree of control may be necessary as a supplement to economic measures or as a means of making incentives workable, but not as a solution in itself. In the countryside there is a great danger of having one costly bureaucracy with massive financial resources – viz. MAFF – paying farmers to do one thing, and another, much weaker, arm of government, the planning system, telling them not to.

One means of taxing intensive agriculture is by positive discrimination against capital investment in farming, almost all of which is directed to increasing intensity of production. This could only be achieved by excluding agriculture from the normal tax incentives for industrial investment. Apart from that, the alternative of taxing the farmer is not feasible since there is no means, except at excessive bureaucratic cost, of determining how output is produced. This leaves us with the option of subsidizing environmentally sound production techniques. A form of this exists in the management agreements with farmers negotiated by the Nature Conservancy Council and the scheme for protecting the moorland in the Exmoor National Park. These management agreements are the main device for protecting the environment under the Wildlife and Countryside Act. They embody three main principles: they apply only to designated high value sites – SSSIs and National Park landscapes; they operate at the point where the farmer proposes to take action which would damage those sites, typically in the course of normal farming operations, and require therefore a notification scheme; and they envisage compensation which is related to the profits forgone if the damaging activity is not carried out.

The basic provisions are embodied in sections 28 and 29 of the Act for SSSIs and in sections 39 and 41 for National Parks. Under section 39 other bodies, e.g. local authorities, have powers to negotiate management agreements for the same purpose.

Under section 28 the Nature Conservancy Council has to notify owners and occupiers of land designated as an SSSI that the land is so designated and tell them what activities would damage the scientific interest of the site, e.g. that valuable plant-rich pasture may not be ploughed, under-drained or treated with nitrogenous fertilizers. If the occupier wishes to carry out such practices then they must give notice of their intention to do so and if the NCC object there is a period of delay of three months during which the NCC may negotiate the payment of compensation.

If the owner or occupier is unhappy with the terms that the NCC offer they may opt for arbitration. Failing agreement at the end of the three-month period, a farmer may proceed to carry out the damaging activity unless in the meantime the NCC has obtained an order under section 29. These orders are made by the Secretary of State on application from the NCC. A section 29 order extends the delaying period by nine months, at the end of which, in the event of failure to reach a management agreement, the NCC may proceed to compulsory purchase and the delay period will be extended as necessary for this.

If a section 29 order is made then the NCC is liable to pay compensation to the owner or occupier not only in respect of any expenditure rendered abortive by the making of the order but also in respect of any loss of income or value of the land resulting from the order. Compensation must also be paid if, as a result of NCC objection, an application for capital grant aid is refused.

At the time of writing, a Department of the Environment working party was determining the principles of compensation but it seems fairly certain that they will be based on the loss of income to landowners resulting from the restrictions on their activities imposed in the interests of conservation. This loss of income may be expressed as a flow, as an annual sum or capitalized into a notional loss of land value. It is basically the difference in value of output less any difference in variable costs, technically known as a difference in gross margin, which would have resulted had the proposed agricultural improvement gone ahead, with adjustment also for any additional capital costs and labour costs (treated as a fixed cost in farm management calculations) that the farmer would have incurred.

The basis of calculation would be the same for voluntary agreements negotiated under section 29 for refusal of grant aid. This form of calculation is embodied in the Exmoor agreements[6] and was the basis of the abortive negotiations for a voluntary agreement between the Broads Authority and the farmers of Halvergate Marshes. As a system for paying for amenity it is perfectly reasonable and practical in principle and, given that agricultural incomes are largely derived from the public purse in any case, it is also equitable that only those farmers whose freedom and hence income is restricted in the interests of conservation and amenity should receive compensation. If society is able to identify those instances where the free choices of producers reduce social welfare and is able, by making payments, to persuade them to act otherwise, then social welfare is improved.[7] But this is not to say that the problem of agricultural policy and the environment is solved by the Wildlife and Countryside Act; it is not. The Act is unacceptable because it is grafted on to the existing system of agricultural policy. Specifically the problems are as follows.[8]

The strongest objections from the conservation lobby were made to the right to compensation in the event of refusal of capital grant aid. Grant aid is in principle discretionary and until administrative changes were made in 1981, largely in order to save civil service manpower, applications for grant aid could be and were refused on a variety of grounds including lack of technical and economic viability. Furthermore, the purpose of these grants is to encourage improvements in agriculture that are thought desirable in the national interest. With SSSIs such improvements are *not* in the national interest: that is the reason for the controls under the Act and indeed the passing of the Act establishes that Parliament, as the arbiter of the national interest, recognizes that this is so. The automatic entitlement to compensation would make sense if grant aid were simply a device for supplementing farm incomes. No doubt the farmers see it that way, as does MAFF, despite official verbiage about the need to increase self-sufficiency and expand agricultural output. The objection to this view is that if, for social purposes, income supplementation is required, it should be given as such without wasting resources on producing unwanted foodstuffs and damaging the environment as well. We return to this question below.

A further aspect of the compensation for refusal of grant aid is that in calculating this compensation as income forgone, it seems likely that subsequent and consequent capital expenditure[9] will be calculated net of grant, i.e. *de facto* farmers will be compensated not only for not receiving a grant for which they have applied but also for grants consequent upon it (which are also in principle discretionary) for which they have not applied; the purpose of all of which is to facilitate an increase in agricultural output which will not take place. This whole absurd situation is avoided if, as we have suggested, grant aid is abolished. Nobody, we imagine, would argue for the farmer to be compensated for not receiving tax allowances for investment that, because of NCC intercession, will not be carried out. This argument is, of course, hypothetical since we do not at present know what the working party will recommend. However, capital costs are calculated net of grant in the Exmoor agreements and it seems most likely that something very similar will be proposed as guidelines under the Act.

This problem, that in compensating the farmers one is compensating them for not receiving future grants, is an aspect of a more general problem of compensation within a highly subsidized agricultural industry. Given that a large proportion of farm income is subsidy, inevitably any compensation for income forgone is to a considerable extent compensation for loss of right to future subsidy. As we have seen, the bulk of farm support takes the form of inflated prices for foodstuffs, maintained by the complex system of import levels and export rebates and monetary compensatory amounts known as the Common Agricultural Policy. Thus much of the subsidy comes from the consumer. A smaller proportion, via AHGS and other schemes, and, in the less favoured areas, stock headage payments, comes from the taxpayer. One effect of preventing farmers on conservation grounds from carrying out farm improvement and compensating them for their consequent income loss is thus to transfer the burden of subsidy from the consumer to the taxpayer.[10] Public expenditure thus rises, but this increase is a gross overstatement of even the financial cost to society of environmental protection. The real cost of this protection is given by valuing the agricultural outputs and inputs at world market prices, i.e. by the value, net of subsidy of the gross margin lost and then allowing for the value of the stream of benefits derived from the amenity. This will be much smaller than the cost of compensation and in some cases, even ignoring values of amenity, where the true value of output is less than the cost of production, will in fact be negative. This will be so for dairying and for the production of sugar beet.[11] Thus in paying compensation within the present system of agricultural protection, the conservation bodies are taking over some of the burden of agricultural support. Because of this, the costs of conservation to them are much greater than the costs to society. Agricultural protection is not their problem and arguably the conservation vote should bear no more than the true costs, in terms of forgone output, of conservation. The major element of compensation, that is agricultural subsidy, should be met by MAFF, or, since most of the savings will accrue to it, by the European agricultural funds, by FEOGA.[12] MAFF will of course experience savings on its expenditure, in so far as section 29 orders or management agreements under section 28 result in fewer payments under AHGS or for livestock headage in the uplands; but because the main burden of support falls on the consumer and not the Exchequer, the savings of expenditure by MAFF will be less than the increase in expenditure by the NCC and the countryside protection agencies.

If the argument above is somewhat convoluted, its implications are straightforward. The system of agricultural support increases the cost of conservation by raising the value of compensation payments. Within a given budget the quantity of conservation that can be done is reduced and the size of the budget necessary to protect a given number of sites is increased, not marginally but by a factor of 3 or 4; in one sample calculation for a wetland drainage scheme, by a factor of 5. Conservation thus appears expensive to the public and its elected representatives when it is in fact not so. What is really expensive is agricultural protection. This not only reduces the NCC's capacity to protect the environment by management agreements and hence increases its reluctance to object to damaging activities; it also renders useless its long-standing last-resort powers of compulsory purchase. For the most part land values are the capitalized income opportunities that the land represents. Agricultural support raises land values and it is broadly these inflated values that the NCC and similar bodies (e.g. the County Naturalist Trusts) must pay if they wish to purchase land.

It is already clear that the NCC budget is nowhere near sufficient for it to carry out its duties of protection of SSSIs under the Act,[13] and there is also evidence that the cost of protection is causing it to withdraw objection from threatened sites:

> our immediate fear was that lacking the finance to pay compensation, NCC would not object to harmful developments on SSSIs. We argued that it must object in every case . . . even if it had no money since that was the only way in which Parliament and the public would be made aware that the fundamental problem lies with the government's continued failure to provide the cash. NCC assured us that this was the line it would take but, in its first test it changed its mind and acceded to the drainage of one of the few remaining wet meadows on Romney Marsh (now a marsh in name only). . . . Apparently they decided not to object, even though they had sufficient money to pay compensation, because they felt that more important sites might be at risk later during the financial year.[14]

The cost of protection would of course be reduced if the proposals for reducing agricultural support and hence prices made in the foregoing pages were carried out. A reduction in support would not only reduce the costs of compensation, bringing them towards the social costs of conservation; by reducing the profits to be made from intensification it would also reduce the pressures on the SSSIs and other valuable areas. In addition, it could be expected to have an impact on a much larger scale than the designated sites and thereby would reduce the danger of environmental deterioration from 'island effects' on small sites within intensive, farmed areas.

A reduction in agricultural support will also obviate another problem caused by the 1981 Act. This is the incentive it provides to owners and occupiers of SSSIs to convert them into income-earning assets by proposing spurious improvement schemes and perhaps applying for grant aid to carry them out,[15] thereby greatly increasing the claims on NCC funds. Reduced support would probably not reduce the incentive to farmers to do this but it would increase the NCC's capacity to cope, both by decreasing the cost of compensation and reducing the volume of genuine proposals. If realistic compensation is paid then it is probably desirable that farmers should exploit the opportunities. Sites would be thereby safeguarded and as a principle it is desirable that farmers should be compensated for conserving the environment.

The present system of support for agriculture has other implications for site protection as facilitated by the Wildlife and Countryside Act. The bias towards arable increases the threat of ploughing compared to other, often less damaging, improvements and increases the cost of defending sites in the lowlands, where the threat is primarily from the plough, relative to those of the uplands. It is significant that the first threat to the efficacy of the Act involved the conversion of marshland to arable.

Not all of agricultural policy is directed at increasing output. The special stock headage payments available in the uplands and remote areas, such as the Scottish Islands, under the EEC Less Favoured Areas Directive, are intended as income supplements to maintain viable communities within these areas.[16] If the intention is income support then it is absurd to provide this in a way which encourages the production of unwanted produce and concomitant environmental damage. Yet this is precisely what the policy of headage payments coupled with generous capital grants does.[17] The policy has achieved considerable success in encouraging increased stocking rates together with pasture 'improvement', farm roads, fencing and field drainage but has failed totally in its prime objective of maintaining viable communities and arresting population decline. Arguably, by encouraging labour-saving agriculture and assisting farm amalgamations, it has made matters worse.[18] The major impact has, of course, been to inflate land values in Less Favoured Areas as the ownership of land in such areas carries with it a licence to receive additional support from public funds.

The more ambitious schemes under the EEC's Integrated Development Programme follow the same faulty logic. That for Outer Hebrides involves a £56 million programme of agricultural improvement and road building of which 60 per cent will come from the UK government. The consequences seem likely to involve draining ecologically rich bogs and the possible destruction of the valuable machair grassland.[19]

The normal objection to simple income supplements on social grounds to farmers in Less Favoured Areas is that they destroy the incentive to improve the viability of agricultural holdings and undermine the self-respect of the recipients. This is nonsense. Headage payments are simply subsidies tied to stock numbers; they do not increase the viability of farms in the areas where they are paid, they simply increase stock numbers and land prices, adding thereby to the problem of disposal of agricultural surpluses and causing, as an unwanted side-effect, environmental damage. If self-respect is undermined by state handouts then it is undermined by the present system, since that is what headage payments are and the farmers are surely not deceived. Replacing headage payments with straight supplementary income subsidies means recognizing that the farmers in Less Favoured Areas perform a socially worthwhile function, maintaining valuable wildlife habitat and landscape, for which they are rightly compensated, and abandoning the myth that they are contributing to national salvation by increasing physical productivity and unwanted livestock products. The objection that richer farmers who do not need income supplements would get them may seem reasonable but is irrelevant since that is exactly what the present system less effectively achieves. Richer farmers are systematically paid more under the present system, whereas income supplements could have an upper cut-off point.

If the aim is to maintain viable rural communities (rather than achieve more efficient farming which would entail much larger and less intensive units) then there is no reason why payments for maintaining traditional farming practices should entail incomes as low as the generally inadequate ones received by the smaller upland farmers under the present system. Certainly where the traditional practices of small farmers are compatible with the environment and multiple use of rural land, incomes should be higher. If society is not faced with a problem of disposing of unwanted livestock produce then it could pay more, especially if it was deriving some environmental benefit at the same time. One qualification is most important, however. Income supplements should not be specific to land and transferable on its sale. If that were the case they would simply get written in to land prices. At most they should be inheritable. Nor should it be possible to use income supplements as collateral to finance agricultural 'improvement'. Rather they should be tied to management agreements, although that might more reasonably be an aim rather than a requirement.

In this book we have quite deliberately avoided discussion of forestry policy and the environmental impact it may have. Large-scale afforestation presents a considerable threat to scarce habitats and valuable landscapes in the uplands,[20] is largely facilitated by tax concession and subsidies, and offers an economic justification which is almost as dubious as agriculture, although some uncertainty exists because, unlike farming, the gestation period of forestry investment is so very long.[21] Any change in the method of agricultural support and particularly, as we recommend, a reduction in the level of protection, will alter the balance of advantage between farming and forestry and lead to pressures for more afforestation. This need not happen in the Less Favoured Areas provided that the average level of income support is not reduced – although it seems likely that controls or other measures are necessary to reduce the present rate of planting there – but falling incomes in the lowlands could well lead to increased planting.

In general this would probably be no bad thing. One solution to the problem of surplus grains would be to put some of the land under a crop of trees, particularly hardwoods in areas with few woodlands. This could be a positive benefit to the environment given proper woodland management. It does not of course mean a permanent loss of agricultural land since timber is no more than a very slow growing crop. Its advantage is that surplus arable land is taken out of arable production for a period until perhaps it is needed and variety is added to lowland landscape and habitats. There has in any case been a serious loss of deciduous woodland in the past decade, as the evidence of Chapter 3 shows.

The danger is that if afforestation increased in the lowlands it would not replace arable but rather increase the pressure on the few surviving ecologically valuable fragments, the residue of SSSIs. In principle the system of habitat protection under the Wildlife and Countryside Act should be sufficient to cope with this pressure, although, as with agriculture, there is a problem of the cost of management agreements when so much of the benefit is in the form of tax concessions and subsidy. As with agriculture the responsibility for paying this element should rest with MAFF.

NCC should pay only the real costs of conservation in the form of output forgone. In general, however, forestry is only agriculture's poor relation in terms of subsidies and since it presents different problems and occupies only one-tenth of the space of agriculture we have deliberately chosen to ignore it rather than deal with the issues at a superficial level.

It is relevant to say that it is our tentative judgement, however, that agricultural reform does not of itself require a reform of the system of grants and tax concessions for private forestry, although a case for reform of these elements probably exists independently of the problem of agricultural protection. The case of public forestry may be somewhat different with its low required rate of return and financial subsidy but a further shift in favour of amenity and environmental quality by the Forestry Commission would probably suffice.

At the centre of our proposals for reform of the system of agricultural support is a reduction in the level of protection and, in consequence, a reduction in the prosperity of agriculture. Given the conditioning to which we have all been exposed from the cradle – from soft cuddly ducks to Beatrix Potter via the Ladybird books,[22] via TV advertisements for country fresh margarine and the endless outpourings from the agricultural lobby and soft sell from politicians – given this conditioning, such a proposal may initially strike the reader as a branch of unthinkable thought, as a proposal so unrealistic that it should immediately be unthought. We shall now briefly try and argue why this is not the case; why the time for this particular thought has come.

In such an argument it is perhaps best to say 'remember the Corn Laws'. The chances of repealing the Corn Laws in 1838 when the Anti-Corn Law League was formed, must have looked far slighter than do the chances of reducing to a tolerable level agricultural protection today. The landed interest was far more entrenched; the urban interest was less organized; society was still very much more feudal and democracy not much more than a dangerous notion. Many of the arguments were almost precisely the same as they are on the agricultural subsidy question today.

Then, as now, scaremongering and xenophobia had a wide currency:

> Supposing then after a time, six or seven millions of our people having become dependent on the United States for bread corn,

those States should be visited with a succession of bad harvests
. . . forcing them to send to Europe for bread corn . . . where
could the corn wanted then be found?[23]

or more alarmist still:

The ruin of this kingdom, which was in vain attempted by
Bonaparte and the Continental Powers under his orders, might
easily be produced by our Legislators rendering England
dependent on Nicholas or Louis Philippe for food. Famine might
starve us into submission and make this nation a province of
Russia or France.[24]

Another familiar strain was the moral quality of the rural versus
the urban coupled with a play on the fear of the unknown:

We are called upon to make the experiment, by which during
the course of this experiment, we should throw out thousands
and thousands of acres from cultivation and bring hundreds of
thousands of industrious people upon the Poor Rates for the
sake of encouraging (and that doubtfully) a class of men whose
lives and habits only lead to misery, decrepitude and infirmity:
– instead of encouraging those whose habits on the contrary
tend to make them good subjects, loyal, well-conducted,
healthy, robust, the main stay of the country.[25]

This argument was even used by Lord John Russell before his
conversion to the anti-Corn Law side:

who wish to substitute the corn of Poland or Russia for our own;
who care not for the difference between an agricultural and
manufacturing population in all that concerns morals, order,
national strength and national tranquillity.[26]

Sir Robert Peel in his speech on Mr Villier's motion on the Corn
Laws (1839)[27] before his change of mind, summarized the
arguments of the pro-protection lobby most coherently from a
conservative viewpoint. His argument essentially was that the
case for repeal had not been made, the claimed benefits would not
materialize and that foreign supplies of corn would not be
available (the alternative claim – that foreign supplies would flood
the market and bring ruin to all farmers and landowners – was
made, but by others). But his peroration is most revealing:

[if the Corn Laws are repealed I would] view with regret
cultivation receding from the hill-top which it has climbed
under the influence of protection and from which it surveys
with joy the progress of successful toil . . . if you [the anti-Corn
Law group] convinced us that your most sanguine hopes would
be realised – that this country would become the great
workshop of the world . . . [then the country] would present the
dull succession of enormous manufacturing towns connected by
railways, intersecting the abandoned tracts which it was no
longer profitable to cultivate – we should not forget amid all
these presages of complete happiness, that it has been under the
influence of protection to agriculture continued for two
hundred years, that the fen has been drained, the wild heath
reclaimed.[28]

The realities, as opposed to the fantasies, of protection and its
repeal, may not have changed, but our attitudes to them have.

When we first suggested cutting back on agricultural support in
1969,[29] we were indeed lonely voices; and we brought down an
intemperate torrent of abuse (amongst the more acceptable things)
on our heads. In 1983 we are now only adding a further faggot to
the pyre on which the CAP will burn. There have been a
succession of books, articles and reports; Shoard,[30] Norton-
Taylor[31] and Body[32] of the polemical variety. There have been
major TV documentaries. There has been a succession of articles
in the serious newspapers. Winning the argument is not difficult.
The present situation is so totally indefensible from every rational
viewpoint: in economic terms, in social terms, in environmental
terms – and even in agricultural terms. The level and effects of
protection under CAP are not just a national scandal; they are a
continental scandal. So one strength we think our proposals have
is rationality in the face of flagrant irrationality and whilst we are
not so naive as to think that rationality ensures a policy is
adopted, we are of the opinion that when the scales are so widely
overbalanced and when such large sums of money are involved,
having an overwhelmingly more rational case which is also more
equitable helps. We believe that almost any objective observer
who can stay awake long enough to absorb the facts of CAP would
see the force of our proposals.

The problem, of course, is that the case is presently not decided
by objective observers. It is decided by the agricultural lobby in

Britain and the EEC and those who may be broadly described as ideologically committed or financially interested. It is decided by the inertia of possession – the ratchet principle discussed in Chapter 4. The interests are obvious. Agricultural land in Britain at the values induced by subsidy is worth in the order of £40 billion. Apart from the assets of landowners, there are the huge interests of the agricultural support industries and the resistance of a whole ministry of civil servants with careers devoted to agricultural support on the line, as well as the associated publicly funded research units and the professional lobbyists.

It must be admitted that supporting this array of interest and inertia there are also still significant ideological structures and political allies of agricultural support. One of the most peculiar things is the support for the farming interest in the Labour party. Farmers vote Tory almost without exception, though there may be a lingering Liberal tradition in parts of Wales and Scotland. Farmers are small, or nowadays often not so small, capitalists yet it was the Labour party that introduced the 1947 Agriculture Act and there is still a powerful feeling in the Labour party that somehow producing food is a morally and socially virtuous activity, whereas the enjoyment of the countryside or a concern for anglers' fishstocks and sport is shameless middle-class frippery. This attitude appears, for a party which if nothing else claims to represent the urban working class and to be interested in equality, totally out of touch with current reality.

In the Conservative party, support for agriculture might seem more in place. There is a streak of romantic Toryism that still sees the yeoman farmer as the backbone of England (probably not of Britain) and rural values as the only ones that are ultimately valid. The Tory party also rightly recognizes its own amongst farmers and is not, at least at present, observably concerned with equity. Active politicians amongst the Tories come from farming backgrounds, as do a few Labour. More, particularly on the Labour side, become farmers and don the ideology when they become successful.

In both parties, however, there are counter forces which are becoming increasingly powerful. In the Labour party there is the growing opposition to the EEC membership, which above all derives its strengths from the perceived iniquities of CAP. It is the urban working-class, cheap food interest asserting itself against romantic visions of pastoral socialism. This force is partially aligned with another traditional strand of Labour thinking, the combination of part of the ethic of the planning profession, essentially a paternalistic aesthetic in this instance, with the access to the countryside lobby rooted in northern England.

If the Labour party should come to power and carry out their present policy of leaving the EEC, it is quite impossible that the level of support for agriculture reported in Chapter 5 could continue. Quite simply even if the Labour party wanted to, realities would not allow it. To secure the aim of cheaper food, there would have to be a switch to some variant of a deficiency payments system and the cost from public funds for the present levels of support would be prohibitive. The Treasury, who have never offered anything warmer than acquiescence to agricultural subsidies, would not allow it. Thus if Labour is elected on anything like its present policies, it is inevitable that the whole system will be reviewed and the level of support drastically reduced.

What can one look for in the Tory party? Here there are two grounds for hope. Although most Tories may be sympathetic to agriculture, they are not sympathetic to subsidies. We already have the Tory Chief Secretary to the Treasury complaining that subsidies to agriculture cost the British taxpayer £1300m in 1982[33] and informed Tory backbenchers, such as Richard Body,[34] writing powerful critiques of agricultural policies. They may be prepared to go on pretending that the import levies are not subsidies since they are not paid from public funds, but the realities of CAP must ultimately catch up with the system. It is the import levies and artificial prices that cause the surpluses and it is the surpluses that cause a large part of the necessary subsidies from public funds, the storage costs, restitution payments, denaturing costs and the others.

The Tories are locked into the EEC and consequently they are locked into a system which can only be radically reformed or explode. Quite apart from being likely to cause a need for ever-growing payments from Community funds to finance the surpluses the system produces, which a strong strand of present Tory thinking is opposed to on principle, the CAP is soon to be overwhelmed by the additional surplus of Greece, Spain and Portugal. The pressure for reform will become irresistible as the European budget becomes totally unmanageable.

In fact one might argue that we are in a classic cycle of protection and approaching the critical point where suddenly the system collapses. A state of affairs which is of very substantial advantage to a few and of only a very minor disadvantage to the many, will continue in existence because the few will lobby for it vigorously whilst the many will take no notice. This state of affairs can go on until the interests of the few begin significantly to irritate the many when the many put a stop to it and repeal the Corn Laws or whatever it may be.

This is exactly the point we are beginning to reach with the CAP. On the one side we have a scandalous level of support creating extreme riches for big farmers but still leaving poor ones poor; generating shameful waste; ravaging the countryside and degrading the rural environment; and disrupting international trade. This has now reached the level where not only are the general public in Europe becoming aware of it but the major western industrial power, the United States, which happens also to be the major world exporter of temperate food products, made it the major issue in the 1982 negotiations on the General Agreement on Tariffs and Trade.

On the other side, we have the growing power of the countryside and environmental lobby documented elsewhere in this book. With that group we have the hard economic logic of the Treasury, regardless of which political party is in power, and the growing anti-EEC sentiment in the country which can only be appeased by sacrificing CAP. The agricultural interest is powerful but it is probably not capable of anything more than token reform of itself. It is not equipped for more. It has been given enough rope and the noose is now slipping over its head. The final factor is, we suspect, simply generational change. We may have been conditioned to accept agricultural support as a fact of life, but each generation tends to right the wrongs bequeathed to it by the previous one (and probably overdo it in the process). The post-Second World War generation reacted to the ills of British agriculture and the financial ruination of many farmers that had set in before the First World War and intensified in the inter-war period. In the process they overdid it and created a new wrong to be righted perhaps forty years later.

If Britain does leave the CAP, which could happen without severing all links with the EEC, the ensuing crisis in CAP, with even less opportunity to off-load its surpluses, would quickly force reform. That would doubtless be to the benefit of conservation in Europe. No doubt the agricultural lobby would wheel out all its spurious old arguments for protection, perhaps with a fresh coat of paint to disguise their weaknesses but probably with no more than a little red lead (or something equally toxic) covering the worst patches of rust. It would be for the conservation and countryside lobby to`join with consumer groups and hard-nosed economists to press for cheaper food and for a lower level of support, a cheaper and more rational agriculture and a tax and subsidy structure designed to protect both the small, poor farmers and the countryside. It might be for the economists to urge a little caution in the speed of rundown of support since with the institutional investment in agriculture and the extent to which farmers have used the asset value of their land as security for borrowing, an overnight rundown might lead to financial collapse and disorder amongst farmers and even far beyond.

With the rundown of the gross level of support to that around the industrial average should go income support to small farmers designed to bring up incomes of farmers with more than say 15 hectares and less than 40, to the national average industrial worker's wage. Whilst it could be that such rights should be transferable by gift, under no circumstances should they be carried as of right with land or be saleable since then their value would simply get capitalized into land prices and their purpose wholly negated. In addition, since the costs of amenity grants would no longer be prohibitive, a range of such grants could be introduced designed to encourage certain agricultural practices compatible with a high quality of countryside and rural environment, and to protect important habitats and encourage farming practices compatible with the extension of such habitats. On the other side, there seems to be no logical case for the exemption of agriculture from rates and a strong positive case for taxing energy used in agriculture on the same basis as that in other industries; and, in addition, taxing certain inputs such as fertilizer and environmentally toxic weed killers and pesticides at a rate which reflected the environmental costs of their use.

These, of course, are general principles for reform in the medium or long term and are aims achievable either inside or outside the EEC. They will not be achieved easily but it is clear that the sheer financial weight of support has made the system unstable and vulnerable and the opposition forces are rising. The political power of farmers in Europe is receding as their numbers decline and the environmental lobby is becoming more powerful. The purpose of this book has been to demonstrate the unity of practical economic common sense with the aims of the environmental and countryside lobby. We hope that in this we may also manage to add just one more touch to the process of demonstrating the invisibility of the emperor's clothes. The ugliness of what then meets a fresh eye will, we believe, provoke a very much more critical appraisal of the agricultural lobby's imperial credibility.

Notes

1 The most recent and complete survey of pension fund holdings to date is by Steel, A. and Byrne, P. J. (1983) 'Financial institutions: their investments and agricultural landownership', University of Reading, Department of Land Management Working Paper no. 1. This estimates the total acreage held by pension funds alone at approximately 340,000 and the total held by financial institutions at 750,000.

2 Davidson, J. (1977) *Conservation and Agriculture*, Chicester, Wiley.

3 For an excellent critique see Caulfield, C. (1981) 'Britain's heritage of wildlife drains away', *New Scientist*, 3 September, pp. 583–6.

4 Shoard, M. (1980) *The Theft of the Countryside*, London, Temple Smith.

5 See Cheshire, P. C. and Leven, C. L. (1982) 'On the costs and economic consequences of planning', University of Reading, Discussion Paper in Urban and Regional Economics, Series C, no. 11.

6 Exmoor National Park Committee, Country Landowners' Association and National Farmers' Union (1981) *Management Agreements in Exmoor National Park*, Dulverton, Devon.

7 Like many economists we here look steadfastly into the abyss of Second Best and step aside!

8 See Bowers, J. K. (1982) 'Compensation and conservation', *Ecos* 3, no. 2, pp. 29–31.

9 E.g. if the application is for grant aid to under-drain a meadow then subsequently for irrigation equipment, farm machinery, grain storage facilities, farm roads, etc.

10 Since the payments by the NCC and the Countryside Commission are out of their Parliamentary grants.

11 See Black, C. J. and Bowers, J. K. (1981) 'The level of protection of UK agriculture', University of Leeds, School of Economic Studies,

Discussion Paper no. 99.

12   In meeting this element of compensation of course neither body would be paying for environmental conservation. To do that they would have to meet the whole of the expenditure.

13   'In our estimation NCC would need about £3 million in 1982/3 to provide it with a realistic ability to enter into management agreements or to purchase land where the owner preferred that option. Apparently, however, NCC sought only £1.2 million and actually received about £600,000', *Birds*, the RSPB magazine, Summer 1982, p. 4.

14   *Birds*, op. cit.

15   As already noted, MAFF has *de facto* abandoned its right to determine the economic viability of grant-aid proposals.

16   Thus in December 1981 in reply to a question on how effective the EEC Less Favoured Areas Directive had been in encouraging production, the Minister replied: 'The principal objective of the Directive is not to encourage production but to compensate farmers in order to ensure the continuity of farming'.

17   Capital grants are at an enhanced rate in Less Favoured Areas – typically 50 per cent against 37.5 per cent elsewhere.

18   MacEwen, A. and M. (1982) *National Parks: Conservation or Cosmetics?*, London, Allen & Unwin.

19   Caulfield, C. (1982) 'Friends the Hebrides can do without', *New Scientist*, 24 June, pp. 862–3.

20   Ratcliffe, D. A. (1980) Memorandum submitted by the Nature Conservancy Council to the Select Committee on Science and Technology (Sub-Committee I – Forestry), Minutes of Evidence, House of Lords, 11 June.

21   See Cheshire, P. C. (1980) 'The economic case for afforestation', paper to 1980 Conference on the Forestry Industry organized by the CPRE; or Bowers, J. K. (1982) 'Is afforestation economic?', *Ecos* 3 no. 1, pp. 4–7.

22   Dahl, R. (1970) *The Fantastic Mr. Fox*, London, Allen & Unwin, provides a recent and welcome exception in childhood reading.

23   Broadhurst, J. (1839) *Reasons for not Repealing the Corn Laws*, London, Ridgway.

24   J.D.C. (1839) *An address to the people of the U.K. on the Corn Laws*, London, Ridgway. (J.D.C. is the abbreviated name used by the anonymous pamphleteer.)

25   J.D.C. (1839), op. cit.

26   Lord John Russell in a letter to a constituent, quoted by Sir Robert Peel in his speech *On Mr. Villier's Motion on the Corn Laws* (1839), reprinted 1839, London, John Murray. This speech preceded Peel's conversion but followed Lord John Russell's.

27 Sir Robert Peel (1839), op. cit.
28 Sir Robert Peel (1839), op. cit.
29 Cheshire, P. C. and Bowers, J. K. (1969) 'Farming, conservation and amenity', *New Scientist*, 3 April, pp. 13–15.
30 Shoard (1980), op. cit.
31 Norton-Taylor, R. (1982) *Whose Land is it Anyway?*, Wellingborough, Northants, Thorsons.
32 Body, R. (1982) *Agriculture: the Triumph and the Shame*, London, Temple Smith.
33 Leon Brittan speaking in Durham and quoted in the *Guardian*, 8 January 1983.
34 Body (1982), op. cit.

Name index

Subject index